D0775516

101 Ways To Save
MONEY

&

SAVE OUR
PLANET

The Green Group:

Barbara Fleishhacker
Patty Friedmann
Loren Werner

Editors:
Kay Radlauer & Werner Riefling

Illustrations & Cover:
Madalyn Dixon

Book Design:
Darrin Harvey

PAPER CHASE PRESS, New Orleans, LA

101 Ways To Save Money
& Save Our Planet

Copyright© 1992 The Green Group

ISBN 1-879706-55-5: $5.95 Softcover
LC: 91-067873

PAPER CHASE PRESS
5721 Magazine St., Suite 152
New Orleans, LA 70115

This was printed on recycled paper
using soybean based ink.

Printed in the United States of America

Acknowledgments

We wish to express our many thanks to the following people who, by their encouragement and invaluable support, helped make this book possible.

Perry Morgan
Lois Falk

Karen Adjmi, Jackie Smith & Liz White,
EarthSavers

Christine Harvey,
Business book author/lecturer,
and money-savings expert

Edi Tshering,
Council on Economic Priorities

L.J. Kairys & Maureen McFalls,
Center for Hazardous Materials Research

Mark Wright,
Association for Commuter Transportation

John Morrill,
Author of several energy-savings books in
connection with the American Council for an
Energy Efficient Economy

Audrey Harthcock
Teresa Bernard

John Mathis
Angela Branch

George Kade
Madalyn Dixon

Nancy Patterson
Porter Wingate
Kate Kolb

Denise Grey
Beth Hanson

Debra Dennis
Al Bloom

Earl Dupre
Bill Erskine

John Booris
Bruce Beck
Matt Lewis
Rose Searing

Penelope Petitte
Neil Ducote

Contents

Household & Garden

1.	Air Freshener	12
2.	All-Purpose Cleaner	14
3.	Biomat Airspray	15
4.	Carpet Spot Remover	16
5.	Cedar Blocks	17
6.	Composter	18
7.	Cotton Fiber Kitchen Towels	19
8.	Detergent	20
9.	Cotton Napkins	22
10.	Dishwashing Liquid	23
11.	Disinfectant	24
12.	Drain Cleaner	25
13.	Fabric Softener	26
14.	Flea Repellent Garlic	27
15.	Floor Cleaner	28
16.	Fly Swatter	29
17.	Furniture Polish	30
18.	Metal Cleaner & Polishes	31
19.	Mosquito Repellent	32
20.	Mouse Traps	33
21.	Oven Cleaner	34
22.	Paper Glue	36
23.	Paper Plates & Cups	37
24.	Paper Towels & Toilet Paper	38
25.	Plastic Food Storage Containers	39
26.	Roach Killer	40
27.	Snail & Slug Killer	41

28. Shoe Polish   42
29. Sponges   44
30. Trash Bags   45
31. Toilet Bowl Cleaner   46
32. Water Soluble Pens or Markers   47
33. Window Cleaner   48

Energy & Water

34. Battery Recharger   50
35. Blow-In Cellulose Insulation   52
36. Caulking & Spackling   53
37. Carpool/Vanpool   55
38. Central Air Conditioning System   56
39. Clothesline   58
40. Compressor   59
41. Dishwasher   60
42. Double or Glazed Windows   62
43. Dryer Exhaust Vent Hood   63
44. Compact Fluorescent Light Bulbs   64
45. Electronic Ballasts   66
46. Enro Heatsaver   67
47. Faucet Aerator   68
48. Gas Appliances   69
49. Gasket Insulators   70
50. Halogen Lighting   71
51. Heating System Tune-Up   72
52. Heat-Pump Heating System   73
53. Heat Traps   74
54. Home Energy Audit   75
55. Low-Flow Shower Head   76
56. Low-Flush Toilet   77

57. Microwave Oven   78
58. Modulating Aquastat   79
59. Occupancy Sensor   80
60. Power Burner   81
61. Programmable Clock Thermostat   82
62. Radiator Vent   83
63. Refrigerator   84
64. Refrigerator Brush   86
65. Refrigerator Door Seal   87
66. Solar Powered Flashlight   88
67. Space Heater   89
68. Squeeze Nozzle   90
69. Tankless Water Heater   91
70. Television   92
71. Toilet Dam   93
72. Volta Batteries   94
73. Wall Switch   95
74. Washing Machine   96
75. Water Bed Heater Timer   97
76. Water Heater Insulating Blanket   98
77. Weatherstrip   99

Personal

78. Clothes with Natural Fibers   102
79. Cosmetics   103
80. Cotton Diapers   104
81. Deodorant   106
82. Soap   108
83. Un-Petroleum Jelly   109

Automotive

84.	Air Pressure Gauge	112
85.	Car Batteries	113
86.	Fuel Efficient Car	114
87.	Rebuilt Engine	115
88.	Recycled Oil Change	116
89.	Retreaded Tires	117
90.	Tuneup	118
91.	VitalizeR	119

Other

92.	Can Crusher	122
93.	Greeting Cards	123
94.	Live Christmas Tree	124
95.	Old Paint Brushes	125
96.	Paint	126
97.	Plants	127
98.	Monkey Globe	128
99.	Products in Glass Jars	130
100.	Unfinished Solid Wood Furniture	131
101.	Recycling Boxes or Bins	132

Sources
135

Index
139

Introduction

The Gallup Organization recently conducted a national survey in which respondents were asked if they would be willing to buy products from companies making an effort to clean up the environment. "Yes," replied 98% of the women and 92% of the men.

People are willing to put their money where their ideology is. Often, though, they labor under a misconception that, as Kermit the Frog once said, "It's not easy being green." Many think that biodegradable products are costly, that recycling is hard to do, that all the conveniences can't be done without. The purpose of this book is to show that the opposite is true: that people can help heal a hurting planet without great effort or sacrifice - **and save money doing it**.

The earth is struggling to survive. Technological advancement often has had a devastating effect on the planet, leaving some parts beyond repair: water sources so polluted by man-made toxins or oil spills that they can never be reclaimed...huge portions of the rainforests destroyed by man's relentless pursuit of material gain, where dozens of species of wildlife have been annihilated...holes in the ozone layer produced by aerosol sprays...it's everywhere you turn.

Are things as bad as they seem? Yes. Is it too late? No.

Many environmental groups, and some publishers, have sought to give the average American direction in helping to prevent further global destruction and to conserve the planet's resources. Books, pamphlets, public forums, talks, workshops: they all put the word out. Education is a vital impetus for action.

It is the hope of the editors that *101 Ways To Save Money & Save Our Planet* can be used as another major educational tool. Its purpose is to show how ecologically responsible behavior does not need to be costly or cumbersome: in fact, there are at least *101 ways* in which it definitely *saves money*. On energy and water bills, on replacement costs, on repairs, on unnecessary disposables, on overpriced toxic products. Everyone can make a difference, however small his contribution. Change for the better comes when more and more people adopt the attitude and actions it takes to make a difference. *101 Ways To Save Money & Save Our Planet* is not the final authority on this subject, but rather it is one more way to motivate people toward change.

The Green Group

Household & Garden

Man manufactures some 70,000 different chemicals throughout the world. Many of these chemicals have not been tested for their effect on people or our planet. And a great number of these chemicals are ingredients for myriad products for household use (i.e., household cleansers, floor cleaners, oven cleaners, soaps, etc.). Apart from the health risks (since many of the chemicals in these products are known to cause cancer), these products usually end up in landfills, drains, or sewage systems. Which means they eventually pollute water supplies.

What is amazing is how chemical companies have very effectively conditioned people to believe that using their toxic and costly products are the *only* way to clean things, or even to clean ourselves. We have been deceived, and can now see the damage of this deception. We have been duped into dumping hazardous products onto our planet, and releasing tons of aerosol propellants into the atmosphere (such as chlorofluorocarbons, CFCs, which deplete the planet-protective layer of ozone surrounding our planet).

Then there is the problem of packaging. Most people do not realize that plastic is not biodegradable. Added to that, plastic is used to package just about any imaginable product. This problem looms large in our society that has condoned quick and easy consumption for so long. Where does it go? In the landfill. Why is that so bad? For one thing, we're running out of room. More than half of this country's landfills in major cities are at capacity!

The following pages list ways you can help save our planet by avoiding various toxic and non-biodegradable products commonly used in homes and gardens, and replace those products with natural, often less costly alternatives. We also identify many items that we can recycle.

1

Air Freshener

Get air fresheners out of your home. You don't need those toxic commercial air fresheners. First of all, they don't really freshen the air. The fact is these so-called "air fresheners" actually line the membrane of your nose with a chemical coating to disguise offensive odors.

The other problem with commercial air fresheners is that you end up throwing out the air freshener packaging. We don't need to add this junk to our burgeoning landfills, nor do we need to add the chemicals (i.e., formaldehyde, phenol, xylene, etc.) left over from the used up air freshener.

If you need to freshen the air, open some windows to ventilate. And if you still feel the need to add some smell to the air, try boiling some lemons, pouring the resulting liquid in bowls, and then placing bowls throughout your home. Lemons have a wonderfully pervasive aroma.

You might even consider getting a product called *Non-Scents*. *Non-Scents* consists of a natural, non-toxic mineral called Zeolite. This mineral literally takes odors out of the air as the result of a chemical reaction. You eventually "recharge" *Non-Scents* out in the sun for a few hours, and use it again, over and over.

Planet Saving Benefit:
By not using air fresheners, you don't use up landfill space, and you don't contribute to adding more toxic chemicals to the planet and its atmosphere.

Money Saving Benefit:
Occasional ventilation is not costly, and a bag of lemons is cheap. No need to buy air fresheners. *Non-Scents* costs $15 for a 1 pound canister, which you may never have to replace.

Where to Get it:

Of course, you can get lemons at supermarkets. But if you still think you need to spend some money on a commercial product, try this source:

Karen's Nontoxic Products
1839 Dr. Jack Road
Conowingo, MD   21918
301/378-4621

Get *Non-Scents* from this source:

The Ecology Box
425 East Washington, #202
Ann Arbor, MI   48104
800/735-1371

2
All-Purpose Cleaner

Get a natural, non-toxic all-purpose cleaner into your home. Anything we can do to avoid using the some 27,000 toxic and hazardous products on retail store shelves is a step in the right direction.

One simple, natural recipe for a non-toxic, all-purpose cleaner is 1/2 cup of washing soda to 1 gallon of warm water. This is very effective for cleaning *all* household surfaces.

Planet Saving Benefit:

When we are not using the toxic products and are using non-toxic products, we are doing the planet and everyone on the planet a favor by not contributing to the toxic dumping which pollutes our water supplies. We also do not expose ourselves to the effect of toxic vapors which we inhale, and which may get in contact with our exposed skin.

Money Saving Benefit:

Washing soda is really cheap compared to the costly toxic products. In fact, 3 1/2 pounds (56 oz.) of washing soda costs about $2 and can last for many months. A typical toxic all-purpose cleaner costs the same, but you only get 12 oz. and this may last perhaps a month or two.

Where to Get it:

Washing soda is in any supermarket or natural food store. If you want to by a commercial, non-toxic and effective all-purpose cleaner through the mail, try this source:

Clean Environments
P.O. Box 17621
Boulder, CO   80308
303/494-1770

3
Biomat Airspray

Get a Biomat Airspray to replace your aerosol spray cans and plastic spray bottles. Most aerosol spray cans are a means to dispense such things as irritants, corrosives, poisons, and other toxins. The propellant of these cans is usually ozone-depleting compounds, packed under at least 40 pounds of pressure, which makes these cans potentially explosive and flammable.

To avoid using any product in an aerosol spray can or bottle, get a Biomat Airspray. The Biomat Airspray is a canister with a pump which you use to build up air pressure. This enables the can to propel planet-safe products (like vinegar for cleaning windows) without risk to yourself or the planet. In fact, the Biomat Airspray will retain the compressed air for up to 2 months.

Planet Saving Benefit:
Aerosol spray cans are usually disposable metal or plastic containers. This means they take up landfill spaces; the plastic spray cans are worse because they are not biodegradable. By getting reusable Biomat Airspray cans, you do not have to throw anything away, which saves on landfill space. Also, you spare our planet's atmosphere from dumping more aerosol propellants or hydrocarbons which produce smog (e.g., pentane and butane). And, you spare our planet's water sources from more toxins that can leak from the aerosol cans.

Money Saving Benefit:
One Biomat Airspray can is cheap: $5. And you can use the Biomat Airspray can over and over for many different things you may want to dispense. It may even be worth the investment to get several of them. Once you use the Biomat Airspray combined with inexpensive, and effective, natural ingredients, you'll never have to squander your money on those expensive, toxic aerosol products again.

Where to Get it:
Get your Biomat Airspray from this mail order source:

Jade Mountain
P.O. Box 4616
Boulder, CO   80306
303/449-6601

4
Carpet Spot Remover

Get a natural alternative to your carpet spot remover. Most spot removers contain a whole slew of toxic chemicals, including some which may be cancer-causing to people.

To remove carpet spots, begin by cleaning up carpet spots the moment they occur. You clean up blood stains with cold water. Use cream of tartar and lemon juice to clean up ink stains. Most non-oily stains can be cleaned up with a solution of 1 teaspoon of white vinegar and 1 teaspoon of plain liquid soap, mixed into 1 cup of lukewarm water.

For most carpet stains, use the natural, non-toxic mineral, borax. Apply as directed on the box.

Planet Saving Benefit:
By adopting natural means to remove carpet spots, we avoid dumping onto our planet such toxins as trichloroethane, ethylene dichloride, naphtha, benzene, and toluene.

Money Saving Benefit:
Borax is not expensive, and is one of those types of things you buy once every few months, usually in a bulk sized quantity. Borax costs about $3 for a five pound box. This is big savings compared to $4 for 1 pound of a toxic product. You can buy vinegar for as little as $1.80 per gallon.

Where to Get it:
Get borax at the supermarket, lumberyard, pharmacy, and some home improvement stores.

5
Cedar Blocks

Get cedar blocks. Most people don't realize it, but those moth balls they have in their closets are very toxic to themselves and to the planet. Moth balls are made from something called paradichlorobenzene. Not only are moth balls highly toxic and unhealthful for you and the planet, they smell funny.

The alternative to moth balls is cedar. Moths hate the smell of cedar and will not get near anything with cedar. Cedar is a wonderful aroma, and perfectly healthful. Put cedar blocks in the drawers where you store clothes, or put blocks in the pockets of clothing hanging in your closet.

Planet Saving Benefit:
Perhaps if no one ever buys another moth ball again, moth balls will not be manufactured, and our usable water source will no longer be threatened by them.

Money Saving Benefit:
Cedar blocks are cheap. It costs about $1 per foot of cedar, 1" X 2". Cedar blocks also last forever, so you may never have to replace them. A good investment.

Where to Get it:
Just go to the local lumberyard and have them cut you several pieces (or however many you need). You can also buy a product called *Cedar Buds*, which is just a $5 bag of 25 1/2" cedar blocks.

These are usually available at home
improvement stores.

6

Composter

Get a composter. Landfills in this country are filling up fast, and there is less and less room to contain all the stuff we throw away. However, it turns out that about 30 to 70% of that stuff can be composted into a rich, usable fertilizer that is better than most commercial products you could buy.

A compost pile is made up of a pile of biodegradable matter. You can throw in such things as wilted lettuce leaves, grass clippings, leaves, etc. This pile then breaks down as it rots and transforms into organic compost or fertilizer. You can then use this fertilizer to add to your garden to produce healthy, lush plants that are usually weed and pest free.

A composter is just a specially designed container in which to create a compost pile. Some composters are made of wood; others are made of recycled plastic.

Planet Saving Benefit:
If we all started to compost most of our garbage, we would use perhaps only half the space for landfills that we now use.

Money Saving Benefit:
Composting is an excellent way for a gardener to save money and have a happy, healthy garden. A gardener using compost can avoid buying expensive fertilizers, and toxic garden pesticides and weed killers.

Where to Get it:
You can get your composter, books, and various accessories from this source:

Gardener's Supply
128 Intervale Road
Burlington, VT   05401
802/863-1700

7

Cotton Fiber Kitchen Towels

Get cotton fiber kitchen towels (ideally, 100% cotton). Americans are great wasters of paper products. Every year we consume nearly a billion trees to produce paper products. Not only that, but when we use paper products, they take up valuable landfill space when we are through with them.

What can we do? Well, we can recycle paper, and that's good. But as far as using paper towels for cleaning things, this is really unnecessary when we can use kitchen towels. Why 100% cotton fiber towels? Because 100% cotton is non-toxic and natural. It won't hurt you and it won't hurt our planet.

Planet Saving Benefit:
When you use cotton kitchen towels instead of those expensive paper towels, you save on the trees it takes to make paper towels, and you do not add to the landfill unnecessarily. Also, fewer paper products means less dangerous toxins like dioxins (a papermaking byproduct) get into the water sources.

Money Saving Benefit:
Cotton towels are not expensive, and they are a one-time investment. You don't need to throw your money away on paper towels anymore. And when they get too ragged, use your old cotton towels as rags.

Where to Get it:
You can get new cotton towels from most department stores. You can probably get cotton towels in very good condition from a thrift shop for as little as 50¢ each. Or you can get some very absorbent 100% cotton fiber towels called *Tuff Towels* for $25.95 per dozen from this source:

Janice Corporation
198 Route 46
Budd Lake, NJ 07828
800/JANICES

8
Detergent

Get a planet safe detergent into your home. Detergents contain phosphates and other toxic things that are not even necessary for cleaning our clothes. In fact, they are harmful to us (may cause cancer in some people) and our planet (pollute our water sources).

For all clothes made of natural fibers (we should try to wear only natural fibers anyway), using natural soap (soap shavings) or borax (a cup per load) in your washing machine will work just as effectively as toxic detergents. And yes, you can even hand wash silk garments. Try it, you may be surprised.

Planet Saving Benefit:
Soap and borax are better products for clothes washing than toxic detergents. You reduce your chance of exposure to something that threatens your health and threatens our planet.

Money Saving Benefit:
Soap and borax are cheaper than toxic commercial laundry detergents. Buy in bulk and save. You can also get biodegradable, non-toxic detergent. *Seventh Generation Laundry Powder* is a phosphate-free, coconut-oil based detergent that costs about the same as most popular toxic commercial detergents, is just as effective, and lasts twice as long (because it is concentrated).

Where to Get it:
You can get borax at supermarkets, drugstores, and some home improvement stores. Natural soaps are available at most natural food stores and ecology shops, or by mail. Try this source:

The Living Source
3500 MacArthur Drive
Waco, Texas   76708
817/756-6341

Get *Seventh Generation Laundry Powder* from:

Seventh Generation
Hercules Drive
Colchester, VT   05446
800/456-1177

9

Cotton Napkins

Get cotton napkins as an alternative to paper napkins. Paper is wasted on all sorts of products. Paper napkins are one of them. Cotton napkins are just as effective as paper napkins, and can last for years. Just use them as you would the paper variety and then throw them in the washer, or hand wash them (it's cheaper that way) for continued use. Why cotton napkins in particular? They are non-toxic, and are usually very absorbent.

Planet Saving Benefit:
Any time we find a natural, replenishable alternative to paper, we save trees. And that is always a good idea.

Money Saving Benefit:
Cotton napkins are a one-time type of investment. Paper napkins are just one more item that will nickel-and-dime your money away. You can get cotton napkins for very little at thrift shops. A dozen may cost $2 to $3. Or get a new set of 8 for around $20 to $30 at a department store.

Where to Get it:
Get cotton napkins at your supermarket, department stores, thrift shops, and specialty shops. Or you can try this mail order source:

Clothcrafters
P.O. Box 176
Elkhart Lake, WI   53020
414/876-2112

10

Dishwashing Liquid

Get a natural, non-toxic dishwashing liquid into your home as an alternative to the toxic one you are now using. One of the several toxins in dishwashing liquid is liquid detergent, which contributes to increasing concentrations of phosphates and other toxins in our water sources. Such a sacrifice is simply too great just for us to get our dishes clean.

As an alternative to the commercial, toxic dishwashing liquids, put shavings from a non-toxic soap bar in a squirt bottle with water. Just use this solution in the same way you would normally use commercial dishwashing liquid.

For dishwashers, use a natural, non-toxic mineral called sodium hexametaphosphate. The name may sound toxic, but it is perfectly safe to us and (as far as we know at this time) our planet. It is also an excellent grease cutting, scale inhibiting replacement for dishwashing detergent. Use sodium hexametaphosphate in the same way you would the toxic variety.

Planet Saving Benefit:
Using natural or non-toxic alternatives to dishwashing liquid or detergent is another good way to prevent further poisoning of our water sources. By avoiding the use of products with detergents, this is also beneficial to a variety of sealife.

Money Saving Benefit:
Soap shavings are usually a little cheaper than dish washing liquid. Sodium hexametaphosphate can be purchased in bulk. One quart sells for $8; 1 gallon sells for $30.

Where to Get it:
Liquid soap is available at any supermarket. Order sodium hexametaphosphate through mail order. Here is one source:

Nigra Enterprises
5699 Kanan Road
Agoura, CA   91301
818/889-6877

11

Disinfectant

Get natural, non-toxic disinfectants into your home. One of the greatest sources of toxins dumped onto our planet comes from products intended for home use. This includes such offensive products as disinfectants. Disinfectants often contain such appalling ingredients as cancer-causing phenol, formaldehyde, and various artificial dyes. There is no need to expose yourself to this and contribute to the ongoing nightmare of toxic dumping.

Here is a simple, very effective alternative: make a mixture of the natural, non-toxic mineral, borax, with hot water. All you need is about 1 cup to each gallon of hot water. Borax will disinfect any household surface. It is also a very effective way to deodorize your home. No more offensive toxic smell.

Planet Saving Benefit:
If you use a borax solution, you can be confident to know once you are through using it, pouring it down the drain will not hurt our planet.

Money Saving Benefit:
Borax is much less expensive than the commercial toxic disinfectants. And since it deodorizes, you won't have to shell out additional money to buy toxic deodorizers.

Where to Get it:
You can get borax at most supermarkets, drugstores, and some home improvement stores. Borax costs about $3 per five pound box.

Buy in bulk and save more!

12
Drain Cleaner

Get a non-toxic drain cleaner or at least get an alternative. Drain cleaners contain lye, which is very harmful to humans (this stuff can actually burn your skin!), and is destructive to our planet. Do not buy drain cleaners, because there are several very effective, less harmful ways to unclog drains. Here are just a couple of methods that work well when your plunger alone doesn't seem to work:

- Pour down your drain a cup of baking soda, followed by a cup of white vinegar, and cover the drain with your plunger. Baking soda and vinegar react together and can dislodge most clogged drains.

- Or you can pour planet-safe and non-toxic 35% hydrogen peroxide down your drain, followed by some vigorous plunging.

Planet Saving Benefit:
Adopting the methods above will not only spare the planet from what may be the worst home product to pour down the drain, but will protect you from accidental spills and obnoxious, unhealthful fumes.

Money Saving Benefit:
Baking soda, white vinegar, and hydrogen peroxide are very cheap compared to high cost drain cleaners. You can use them for drain cleaning, and for many other applications as well. A bottle of hydrogen peroxide costs merely 40¢ for 16 oz. versus $2.50 for 12 oz. of highly toxic Drano™. Get a gallon of vinegar for only $1.80, and it'll last a long time. Baking soda should cost no more than $3 for a 5 lb. box.

Where to Get it:
These ingredients can be found at most supermarkets. If you want to buy a commercial, non-toxic drain cleaner, try this mail order source:

Clean Country
P.O. Box 448
Willmar, MN   53201
800/448-1999

13

Fabric Softener

Get rid of your commercial, toxic fabric softener and use a natural alternative. Fabric softeners contain such obnoxious ingredients as ammonia and synthetic fragrances. The fact is you do not need these fabric softeners to soften your natural fiber clothes.

Try using 2 cups of white vinegar in 1 full tub of rinsewater. This should get your clothes fluffy. Drying them on a clothesline can also help make clothes fluffy and clean smelling. Don't mix vinegar with chlorine bleach or you produce noxious and dangerous fumes. As an alternative to vinegar, you can use a cup of baking soda for each wash load. When do you add the baking soda? Add it as you load your washer. The baking soda will make your clothes fluffy.

Planet Saving Benefit:
By not using fabric softeners you keep the toxic chemicals, and the plastic bottles they come in, out of landfills.

Money Saving Benefit:
Vinegar and baking soda are cheap. So is a clothesline.

Where to Get it:
You can get vinegar and baking soda from any supermarket. If you want to buy a natural, non-toxic fabric softener, try this source:

Mountain Fresh
P.O. Box 2000
Grand Junction, CO
81504
303/434-8434

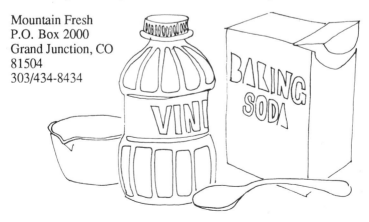

14

Flea Repellent Garlic

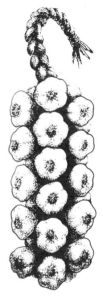

Get garlic to repel fleas from your pet in place of toxic flea repellent. Toxic flea repellent is just another source of pesticide to pollute our planet. Pesticides tend to just seep into our water tables. A good way to keep fleas away is to simply add garlic to your pet's diet. Try adding minced or crushed garlic and mix well into your pet's food. Try half a clove to every cup of food. You may increase or reduce the dosage according to the strength needed to fend off the fleas.

Believe it or not, your pet can become a garlic lover just like most garlic eating people. Garlic will not only keep the fleas away, as the garlic scent exudes from your pet's skin, but may keep your pet healthier since garlic provides added nutritional value. You may try to make garlic a regular part of your diet, too. Ask your doctor or nutritionist about the advantages of eating garlic regularly.

Planet Saving Benefit:
When you use garlic to repel fleas, you are not using toxic pesticides to get rid of fleas. Garlic is good for you, your pet, and our planet.

Money Saving Benefit:
Garlic can be grown in your garden, which means you will have a free supply. Or you can buy garlic cheaply in bulk.

Where to Get it:

Most supermarkets have garlic in their produce departments.

15
Floor Cleaner

Get a natural alternative to your commercial, toxic floor cleaner. Many floor cleaners contain ammonia and other toxic ingredients. Just as for any other surface in your home, you can use a planet-safe alternative. What follows is a list of ways to clean different types of floors:

• *Brick or stone floors.* Mix 1 cup of white vinegar with 1 gallon of water. Brush scrub floor with this solution and rinse with water.

• *Ceramic tile.* Mix 1/4 cup (or more) white vinegar with 1 gallon of water. Brush scrub floor. Won't leave film.

• *Linoleum.* Mix 1/2 cup white vinegar with 1/2 gallon water. Wash away dirt and grime with a mop.

• *Wood floors.* Mix 1 part vegetable oil and 1 part vinegar. Apply this solution to the floor as a thin coat. This solution cleans and shines your floors.

Planet Saving Benefit:
As long you use natural ingredients for floor cleaning, you are not dumping toxins down the toilet and into our planet's water table.

Money Saving Benefit:
Vinegar and vegetable oil are cheap. Vinegar costs about $1.80 for a gallon. These ingredients are certainly cheaper than expensive and toxic floor cleaners. Biodegradable floor cleaners are available. For example, you can get the *AFM-35 Super Clean* biodegradable floor cleaner. This sells for about $6 per quart.

Where to Get it:
Get vinegar and vegetable oil at most supermarkets. If you want to get the *AFM-35 Super Clean* floor cleaner, contact this source:

AFM Enterprises
1140 Stacy Court
Riverside, CA   92507
714/781-6860

16

Fly Swatter

Get a fly swatter. Like cockroaches, ants, and mosquitoes, flies sooner or later become a bothersome presence in your life. Unfortunately, many of us make the mistake of getting a can of highly toxic insect killer and start spraying up a storm. This is not only hazardous to people, but hazardous to our planet when toxins finally settle on our planet's surface. Alternative: the fly swatter. You know, the thing with a long handle and a flat spatula-like end with holes in it. The fly swatter flattens flies very effectively. Sometimes wielding a shoe will work, but it's not what you want to go slamming against your walls.

Planet Saving Benefit:
As long as you use a fly swatter, you probably won't use an insect killer (or at least we hope you don't). No insect killer means fewer toxins dumped onto our planet.

Money Saving Benefit:
Fly swatters are much cheaper than any insect killer will ever be. Plus, unlike insect killer, fly swatters will last forever.

Where to Get it:

Get fly swatters at supermarkets, pharmacies, and lumberyards, etc.

17

Furniture Polish

Get a natural alternative to your toxic furniture polish. Furniture polish contains any number of toxic chemicals including some potential cancer-causing chemicals like phenol, naphtha, and nitrobenzene. These are some of the most hazardous chemicals plaguing our planet. None of them are necessary for the main goal: to get the wood of your furniture to absorb oil.

There are several effective alternatives to furniture polish:

• Mix 3 parts olive oil and 1 part vinegar. Apply with a cloth.

• Mix 2 parts vegetable or olive oil and 1 part lemon juice. Apply with a cloth.

The oil and lemon mixture makes your furniture look and smell great.

Planet Saving Benefit:
Go natural, and forget the toxic commercial stuff. We definitely do not need any more hazardous chemicals ruining our planet.

Money Saving Benefit:
Olive oil, vegetable oil, vinegar, and lemons are all cheap, especially when compared to those expensive, toxic furniture polishes. Furniture polish can cost you $3 for 12 oz. Vegetable oil only costs about $1.20 for a 24 oz. bottle.

Where to Get it:
The natural ingredients mentioned here are all available at your supermarket. For a commercial, natural furniture polish, try this source:

Eco-Choice
P.O. Box 281
Montvale, NJ   07645
201/930-9046

18

Metal Cleaner & Polishes

Get a natural alternative to your toxic metal cleaner and metal polisher. Metal cleaners and polishers contain such planet assaulting chemicals as petroleum products, ammonia, and synthetic fragrance. There are several non-toxic alternatives you can adopt for various metals. Here are a few:

*   *Brass.* Rub brass with olive oil on a dampened cloth. Worcestershire Sauce also works effectively to polish brass when applied in the same way.

*   *Bronze.* Put 1 teaspoon salt into 1 cup of white vinegar to dissolve the salt. Then add flour and mix to make a paste. Apply the paste to the bronze item and let sit for 1/2 hour. Rinse off the mixture with warm water and polish with a dry cloth.

*   *Chrome.* Wipe chrome with a cloth dipped in white vinegar.

*   *Copper.* Rub copper with a slice of lemon sprinkled with baking soda. Then rinse the copper with water and dry with a cloth.

*   *Gold.* Wipe gold with a cloth dipped in lukewarm soapy water. Then dry the gold with a dry cloth.

*   *Silver.* Make a paste of baking soda and water, then apply to the silver. Rub the silver, rinse the silver with water, and dry the silver off with a dry cloth.

Planet Saving Benefit:
Use natural alternatives to the toxic version of metal cleaners and polishers, and you avoid throwing away toxins.

Money Saving Benefit:
Olive oil, white vinegar, baking soda, and lemons are not a major investment. Spending your money on commercial, toxic metal cleaners and polishers is not worth the investment.

Where to Get it:
The ingredients listed here are all available at your local supermarket.

19
Mosquito Repellent

Get rid of your toxic mosquito repellent. Mosquito repellents, like all insect repellents, contain highly toxic pesticides. Pesticides are not good for you (especially when inhaled), and usually end up in our water sources.

How can you repel mosquitoes? First try to prevent them from living near your home. You can do this by eliminating pools of stagnant water, and by planting the herb basil in your garden. Mosquitoes don't like the scent given off by basil. When you are in your backyard, you can burn natural citronella candles. Citronella candles contain oils derived from citronella, which is a fragrant grass grown in southern Asia.

Another good idea is to avoid attracting mosquitoes. You do this by not wearing floral prints, bright colors, bright jewelry, or sweet scented perfume.

If you live in an area where mosquitoes are known to cause encephalitis, malaria, or some other disease, get out of that area! Fortunately, in the United States the incidence for such diseases is fairly rare. If you can't leave, a more toxic repellant may be warranted.

Planet Saving Benefit:
Don't get mosquito repellent; there are too many pesticides dumped onto our hurting planet already. The alternatives mentioned can not only keep mosquitoes away, but can actually help the planet (such as planting fragrant, edible plants like basil).

Money Saving Benefit:
When you don't have to buy can after can of insect repellent, and instead adopt a few sensible practices, you may not have to spend any money when dealing with mosquitoes.

Where to Get it:
If you want to get citronella candles, you can try your local lumberyard or nursery.

20
Mouse Traps

Get mouse traps (the old fashioned wooden variety) instead of using the toxic, poisonous way to kill mice. Mouse traps still work very effectively. And you can use them over again. Of course, if the idea of killing a mouse appalls you (which it does us), get a *Seabright Humane Mousetrap*. This mouse trap was specially designed (it looks like a see-through house) to catch a mouse alive and unharmed, to be released free outdoors.

Planet Saving Benefit:
Mouse traps are made of wood and metal, and can be incinerated if thrown away. This means they will not take up valuable landfill space. The *Seabright Humane Mousetrap* is such a neat idea, you won't want to throw it away; it costs about $10.

The important thing is that by not using toxic mouse poison, you keep one more source of toxins out of the environment, and leave a little room in the landfill.

Money Saving Benefit:
Conventional mouse traps and the Seabright mouse traps are inexpensive and can be used for years. They are much cheaper than buying poison or hiring an exterminator.

Where to Get it:
Get mouse traps at nearly any hardware store. You can get the *Seabright Humane Mousetrap* from this source:

Humane Alternative Products
8 Hutchins Street
Concord, NH 03301
603/224-1361

21

Oven Cleaner

Get a natural alternative to your toxic oven cleaner. Many people just neglect to maintain a clean oven, and let things build up. And when things get bad enough, they buy a commercial product that contains a highly corrosive toxin: lye. Why these types of products are sold at all is beyond understanding. Often people get severe chemical burns when this product comes in contact with exposed skin. Lye is also very hazardous to eyes or internal organs (especially if the product is inhaled).

The worst danger comes from oven cleaners in aerosol spray form. The can which contains the product is highly explosive and flammable, and the propellant could be some form of hydrochlorofluorocarbon (HCFC) or some other hydrocarbon compound which poses a threat to our environment. HCFCs react with and reduce the ozone layer of our planet's atmosphere and hydrocarbons, like pentane or butane, add to greenhouse gas pollution.

There are several safe, natural ways to clean your oven. Sprinkle salt over a spill in your oven while the oven is still warm. A dry spill should be moistened, and salt sprinkled over the spill. After the oven has cooled, scrape the spill away, using a dry sponge or cloth.

If you have some tough spots in your oven, equip yourself with baking soda and fine steel wool. With the oven cool, first wet the surface, then sprinkle a layer of baking soda over the area which needs cleaning. You can now wipe clean most of the oven using a dry sponge or cloth. Get those tough spots out using the steel wool, and wipe clean.

To maintain your oven, you can wipe it out regularly with a cloth dampened with vinegar.

Planet Saving Benefit:

Avoid anything that contains an aerosol propellant such as HCFC, pentane, or butane and avoid anything that contains lye. Lye which is either derived from sodium hydroxide or potassium hydroxide, is dangerous to people, and is toxic to our planet. This stuff will eventually seep down to our water sources like most of the other toxic junk.

The natural alternatives spare us and our planet from all these terrible things.

Money Saving Benefit:
Baking soda, vinegar, and steel wool are cheap compared to highly toxic oven cleaner.

Where to Get it:
Anything you need to clean your oven you can usually find at the supermarket.

22

Paper Glue

Get a natural alternative to your toxic, commercial glue. Most glues contain such things as ammonia or ethanol as solvents, and a whole host of carcinogens like formaldehyde, phenol, and even vinyl chloride, which is really bad stuff. These highly toxic ingredients are usually found in airplane glue, instant glues, super glues, whatever. Whenever possible, it is best to get glues that are relatively safe, like white glue. Or you can make your own glue.

To make your own, non-toxic paper glue, perform this procedure:

• Mix 3 tablespoons of cornstarch with 4 tablespoons of cold water, and make a smooth paste.

• Now boil 1 1/2 cups of water and stir the paste into the water.

• The mixture should become clear. Use when the mixture is cool.

Planet Saving Benefit:
Any time we use a natural, non-toxic glue over a highly toxic glue, we spare our planet from the further toxic pollution of our water sources.

Money Saving Benefit:
Most natural glues are very effective. Moreover, they are cheaper than the toxic variety of glue. The cornstarch glue is useful for many applications where glue is needed. Make some and keep it around the house in a closed jar. It's cheap, easy to make, and lasts a long time when stored in your refrigerator.

Where to Get it:
White glue is a good, mostly safe glue. You can get white glue at most art supply stores, hardware stores, supermarkets, and stationery stores. If you wish to get a commercial, non-toxic, and very effective glue, you can try this source:

Livos Plantchemistry
1365 Rufina Circle
Santa Fe, NM   87501
800/621-2591

23
Paper Plates & Cups

If you feel the need to use disposable plates and cups, at least use recycled/recyclable paper plates and cups. Most of us don't think about the tremendous hazard posed by something as seemingly harmless as picnic plates and cups if they are made from Styrofoam. Styrofoam is terrible stuff. Why? Because Styrofoam never goes away. Yes, that means the plate you used for that barbecued chicken dinner you had ten years ago is still sitting on some landfill somewhere. And will sit there forever, probably.

What is Styrofoam? Its made from cancer-causing benzene, which is used to produce styrene, which is then blown up usually with HCFCs to create a foam. HCFCs, of course, are known to destroy the ozone layer in the atmosphere which protects our planet.

The moral is this: don't get Styrofoam plates, cups, or anything. Instead, get recycled/recyclable paper plates and cups. Of course, we would rather that you avoid anything disposable in the first place.

Planet Saving Benefit:
It is always better to get paper when a paper alternative exists to any product made of Styrofoam. Unfortunately, when you are through using paper plates and paper cups, you probably can't add them to your recycling bin. The reason is that paper plates and paper cups usually have a laminate or coating on them. This coating makes it difficult to recycle. However, the paper plates and paper cups will eventually break down, unlike their Styrofoam counterparts.

Money Saving Benefit:
Paper plates and paper cups should cost less than Styrofoam plates and cups.

Where to Get it:

Get paper plates and cups from
nearly any supermarket.

24

Paper Towels & Toilet Paper

Get paper towels and toilet paper made of recycled paper. Paper is a commodity that too many people take for granted in this country. Each of us consumes nearly 600 pounds of paper per year. Admittedly, paper is a hard thing to live without. Much of the paper is just used to package the things we buy (up to about 30% of our garbage). A lot of paper is used to make the newspapers we read and unsolicited junk mail we receive.

What to do? There is no reason not to get paper towels and toilet paper that has been manufactured from recycled paper. Of course, we would rather that everyone just skip using paper towels altogether and use cotton cloth towels instead.

Planet Saving Benefit:
As part of our effort to avoid wasting paper, using paper towels and toilet paper made from recycled paper is a good practice to adopt.

Money Saving Benefit:
Paper towels and toilet paper made from recycled paper may not always be cheaper. But in some cases, the product is made better, and you actually get more for your money. It is best to get a product which does not have "cushions." These "cushions" are just a tricky way for the manufacturer to create the illusion that you are getting more for your money when you really are not.

Where to Get it:
Get recycled paper towels and toilet paper from most supermarkets. Check the packaging to see if the product has been recycled.

Look for the recycled symbol and
the word "recycled."

25

Plastic Food Storage Containers

Get plastic food storage containers. Normally we would not encourage the use of plastic. It's bad enough that even good, natural products come in plastic packages. In fact, about 1/3 of all packaging, regardless of the product, is made of plastic. This country uses more than 50 billion pounds of plastic annually. Why not plastic? Plastic is another substance that uses petroleum, and is another substance that takes up landfill space because it is not biodegradable.

However, if used wisely, plastic can be a good thing. For example, for food storage. Now many people use plastic wraps to store food. The problem here is that plastic wrap is intended to be used once and thrown away. That works against the environment. Rather, if you need to use plastic for food storage, get some containers with tight-sealing lids to use over and over again. In other words, get something you won't use once and throw away.

Planet Saving Benefit:
The careful use of plastic, or better yet, less use of plastic, reduces the amount of petroleum used and the landfill space occupied by something that just won't go away.

Money Saving Benefit:
Buy plastic containers you plan to use over and over again. This makes them one-time investments. And since they do not really wear out, or break down, they can be passed down from generation to generation. Plus, plastic containers are usually cheap, especially when compared to plastic wrap. For example, one 2 quart plastic Rubbermaid™ container costs $2.45, while one disposable roll of plastic wrap costs $3.

Where to Get it:
Get plastic containers with tight-sealing lids at your supermarket or department store.

Rubbermaid™ makes good plastic containers often available in supermarkets.

26
Roach Killer

Get a natural alternative to your commercial, toxic roach killer. No one likes roaches. And sooner or later, you'll want to kill one that has invaded your domicile. The problem is that they seem to be the hardest pests to kill. You slam them with a shoe and they seem to hobble away as if you did nothing.

Whatever you do, don't use the pesticide based roach killers! Instead, try this clever method: mix equal parts of baking soda and powdered sugar, and put this concoction in the infested area. The little rascals eat this stuff, and have a bad case of gas, which kills them. Just sweep their carcasses up and toss them away. Yes, roaches are biodegradable.

Planet Saving Benefit:
Toxic roach killer may kill roaches, but the toxins are also killing our planet. By continuing the use of shoes or this special, natural meal recommended here, you do no harm to yourself or the planet.

Money Saving Benefit:
Baking soda and powdered sugar are not expensive. Shoes can be expensive, but a cheap old tennis shoe that you are going to throw out anyway can be effective.

Where to Get it:
You can get baking soda and powdered sugar
at your supermarket.

27

Snail & Slug Killer

Get a natural alternative to your snail and slug killer. Not everyone has snails and slugs to kill. But those of you who do may think you have no alternative but to use snail and slug food, which is just a pesticide in edible form for these pests.

Try this effective way of ridding your garden of these pests: pour some stale beer into a dish and set the dish out in your garden. If your dog doesn't get to it first, the snails and slugs will be drawn to the sweet scent of the beer, take a dip, and drown.

Planet Saving Benefit:
You don't need to get commercial snail and slug killer, which could just end up seeping into our planet's water table.

Money Saving Benefit:
Stale beer is cheaper than snail and slug killer. If you don't drink, ask a neighbor. Someone, somewhere will have a can of the stuff sitting around growing stale somewhere around his home. You can also get a slug trap called the Slug Saloon™. This product employs the same method presented here, but keeps your dog out of the bait. Each trap costs $6.

Where to Get it:
Get your own Slug Saloon™ from this source:

Gardens Alive
Highway 48
P.O. Box 149
Sunman, IN   47041
812/537-8650

28

Shoe Polish

Get a natural alternative to replace your toxic, commercial shoe polish. Shoe polish is a highly toxic substance produced from several known cancer-causing chemicals like trichloroethylene, methylene chloride, and nitrobenzene. These can be easily absorbed through your skin if they make contact with your skin, and they are easily absorbed by our planet to seep into our drinking water sources.

There are several natural, non-toxic alternatives. Try any of these methods:

- Apply olive oil to leather shoes of any color and buff to a shine with a soft cloth.

- Apply lemon juice to black or tan leather shoes and buff to a shine with a soft cloth.

- Apply cool black coffee to black suede shoes by rubbing in the coffee with a sponge.

- Apply white vinegar to patent leather with a soft cloth moistened with the vinegar.

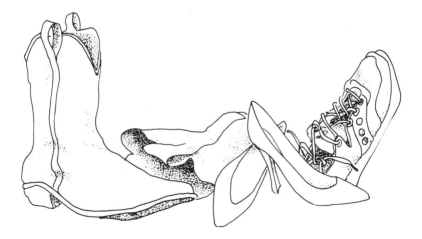

There are, of course, natural, commercial shoe polishes available.

Planet Saving Benefit:
Avoid introducing carcinogens to landfills and into our water supply by adopting these simple natural alternatives to keeping your shoes shined.

Money Saving Benefit:
Such things as small amounts of olive oil, lemon juice, coffee, and white vinegar are far cheaper than costly shoe polishes. A natural commercial shoe polish can be a good investment. AFM puts out the *AFM-31 E-Z On Shoe Polish* for white, black, and brown leather shoes. This sells for about $12.75 per pint.

Where to Get it:
Your supermarket has all you need for shoe polish. However, if you wish to get a natural, commercial product, try this source:

The Living Source
3500 MacArthur Drive
Waco, TX   76708
817/756-6341

29
Sponges

Get natural sponges. Sponges are a handy thing to have around your home. But the commercial sponges you get at the supermarket are usually made from polyurethane, which is derived from petroleum. Petroleum, of course, is a diminishing natural resource which we must learn to conserve. Besides that, polyurethane is not biodegradable. So, when polyurethane sponges end up at your landfill, they just sit there and never go away.

Some people who want to use natural products think the logical alternative is to use sea sponges. Sea sponges may be non-toxic, but they too are a diminishing natural resource. What's a good planet saving alternative? Sponges made from wood pulp cellulose.

Planet Saving Benefit:
Cellulose sponges are biodegradable. That way, when you throw them out, they will go away, unlike the polyurethane variety of sponges. And they're plentiful, unlike the sea sponge, which could be depleted.

Money Saving Benefit:
Cellulose sponges are a good investment because they are usually thicker and more absorbent than the polyurethane sponges, and they are cheaper. You can get 10 rectangularly shaped sponges with these dimensions: 4" x 3" x 3/4", for about $6.

Where to Get it:
You may find cellulose sponges at natural food stores and ecology shops. Or you can get them through this mail order source:

Seventh Generation
49 Hercules Drive
Colchester, VT   05446
800/456-1177

30

Trash Bags

Get recycled/recyclable paper trash bags. One of the problems with the growing volume of garbage filling up in this country's landfills is the problem of the plastic bags used to transport that garbage. Plastic does not break down. It just sits there and takes up space. Efforts have been made by various companies to produce biodegradable bags. However, not all bags break down fully, so they still pose a threat to our water sources and land fills.

What can you do? Use recycled/recyclable plastic trash bags, or preferably use recycled/recyclable paper trash bags.

Planet Saving Benefit:

If you use recycled/recyclable plastic trash bags, it is possible to get plastic bags made from up to 80% recycled plastic. Using this type of plastic bag reduces the amount of new plastic needed to make new plastic bags.

If you use recycled/recyclable paper bags, you don't have to worry that these will harm the planet, because they will break down.

Money Saving Benefit:

You can save on both plastic and paper bags if you buy them in bulk.

Where to Get it:

You may need to check out a home improvement or office supply store (both should probably be the warehouse variety) to get bulk savings. To get 9 to 30 gallon paper trash bags, contact this source:

Set Point Paper Company
31 Oxford Road
Mansfield, MA   02048
508/339-9300

31

Toilet Bowl Cleaner

Get an alternative to your toxic toilet bowl cleaner. Toilet bowl cleaners are just another of the many household cleaning products that contain toxic, people- and planet-harming chemicals. Don't buy them, because you don't need them.

To clean stubborn grime, like the toilet bowl ring, make a paste of borax and lemon juice and apply this paste to the ring. Let the mixture sit there for about 2 hours. Afterwards, scrub the ring away.

To maintain a clean toilet bowl, sprinkle baking soda and then vinegar into the bowl. Scrub the bowl to clean and deodorize.

Planet Saving Benefit:
If you don't use a toxic toilet cleaner, you spare the planet from more toxic chemicals.

Money Saving Benefit:
Borax is cheap in bulk, and baking soda and vinegar are not major investments. Time, energy, and *money* are saved by just maintaining the toilet.

Where to Get it:
Get borax at the supermarket, lumberyard, pharmacy, and some home improvement stores.

32

Water Soluble Pens
or Markers

Get non-toxic water soluble pens or markers. Most commercial pens or markers are unbelievably toxic. In fact, a majority of the ingredients of toxic pens and markers are carcinogenic, including such things as naphtha, phenol, and toluene. Not only do they pose a threat to the user, but since these things are intended to be thrown away, they pose a big threat to our planet when they seep into our water sources.

You can avoid unnecessary exposure to toxic pens and markers by just buying only water soluble pens and markers. They come in any color imaginable, and can be used for nearly any application for which the toxic variety is used.

Planet Saving Benefit:
Non-toxic pens or markers mean fewer cancer-causing toxins are dumped into landfills and into water sources.

Money Saving Benefit:
Water soluble pens and markers can be cheaper than the toxic variety. This is mainly because the toxic variety simply cost more to manufacture. Also, you save yourself the expense and trouble of going to a doctor, since you probably won't react to the water soluble ink; many people have allergic reactions to the toxic inks.

Where to Get it:

Get non-toxic pens and markers from many art supply stores, ecology stores, and stationery stores.

33
Window Cleaner

Get a natural alternative to window cleaner into your home. Commercial, toxic window cleaners usually contain ammonia or isopropyl alcohol. If ammonia happens to get mixed with bleach you end up with an extremely corrosive solution. Ammonia alone in high concentrations can cause severe burns.

The other problem with commercial window cleaners is the packaging. Window cleaners usually come in a plastic bottle with a spray nozzle.

You do not need window cleaner in your house. All you need is planet-safe, white distilled vinegar. Vinegar will cut through practically any grime you could have on your windows. If you wish, you can dilute the vinegar in lukewarm water (try 1/2 cup of vinegar to every gallon of warm water) and maybe even add a little lemon juice. Just wipe on this solution with a cloth and then use your squeegee.

Planet Saving Benefit:
Vinegar will not harm anything; ammonia will. Also, by not buying a commercial window cleaner, you will not be dumping the plastic bottles into landfills. A suggestion: if you already have one, put a solution of vinegar into the plastic bottle and use it that way.

Money Saving Benefit:
Vinegar is very inexpensive, and when you make a diluted solution of vinegar and water, vinegar can be stretched a long way for window washing. You should not pay more than $2 per gallon of vinegar.

Where to Get it:
Get vinegar at most major supermarkets.

Energy & Water

This part of the book lists ways you can get products or identify professional services that can help you save energy and water, and save you money at the same time.

Energy

The choices we make to use energy can have an impact on the planet's health beyond than any other environmentally related matter. The misuses of the planet's energy sources have resulted in such atrocities as acid rain, global warming, oil spills, radioactive waste, smog, strip mines, and so on.

You can do a lot to make sure you are not adding more to the misuse of energy. For example, any time you buy a major appliance, you are, in effect, committing yourself to absorbing a certain percentage of energy over time. Obviously, if you end up buying an energy hog, you end up wasting energy.

And if that is not particularly disturbing, consider this: an energy hog is not only hurtful to the planet and the atmosphere around the planet, but hurtful to your pocketbook. The fact is, getting a cheap appliance without concern about its energy efficiency is actually a lousy investment. You will spend more for the energy used to operate the appliance than the amount paid to buy the appliance in the first place.

Water •

For the most part, water is peculiar only to this planet. Most other planets have either no water, or virtually none. And without water, life really could not exist on this planet. Water is precious. However, as far as water relates to humans, only a small part of all the water on this planet is drinkable: about 1%. And most of that percentage is either above or beneath the surface of the planet. In this country, more than half the population depends on water from beneath the surface, natural water tables. Unfortunately, water sources, above and beneath, are being polluted beyond the point that they ever can be used again.

You must learn to do two things: stop wasting water, and stop dumping toxins onto the planet's surface that can pollute the water sources above and seep to the water sources beneath the surface of the planet.

Addressed in this part of the book are some effective ways to prevent wasting the precious water supply, whatever its source.

34

Battery Recharger

Get a good battery recharger. If you decide to buy non-disposable, rechargeable batteries over the low-toxin Volta batteries (described elsewhere in this book), make sure you get the best, long lasting rechargeable batteries available, and the best recharger available.

The best batteries and recharger we know of on the market today are made by a company called Millennium. Millennium™ batteries are guaranteed to last 1,000 times longer than any major name brand, and they hold their charge up to 33% longer than any major brand. These are some serious batteries. The Millennium™ recharger is also a serious recharger. The Millennium™ recharger recharges any rechargeable battery in just 3 hours. That out-performs most rechargers that take 2 to 4 times as long to recharge batteries.

Planet Saving Benefit:

The mercury and other heavy metals often used in batteries have been the main source of heavy metal pollution in our planet's landfills. We want to avoid contributing to this source. Why? Because these metals invariably seep into our planet's water table.

If you get very good batteries and a very good recharger, you use fewer heavy metal batteries. Therefore, when it comes time to throw those batteries away, you throw fewer batteries into the local landfill. Fortunately, Millennium has set up programs to recycle their batteries. A good planet saving idea.

Money Saving Benefit:

Long lasting, rechargeable batteries and an efficient battery recharger are a good investment. Now, the initial purchase of Millennium™ batteries may seem high. But when you consider they will last a lot longer than all the other batteries on the market, you come out ahead. Besides, you save on the hassle of having to replace batteries every few weeks. Examples of cost: 2 AAA Millennium™ batteries are $7.95; 2 C Millennium™ batteries are $9.95; 2 D Millennium™ batteries are $9.95. The Millennium™ Ni-cad Recharger is $25.95.

Where to Get it:

Get Millennium products at many electronic stores, home improvement stores (the warehouse variety), and department stores. Seventh Generation has a program to recycle Millennium™ batteries. Contact Seventh Generation here:

Seventh Generation
49 Hercules Drive
Colchester, VT 05446-1672
800/456-1177

NOTE: Don't fret if you're put on hold when calling Seventh Generation; rather than being assaulted by elevator music, you get to listen to a wonderful recording of a babbling brook and singing birds.

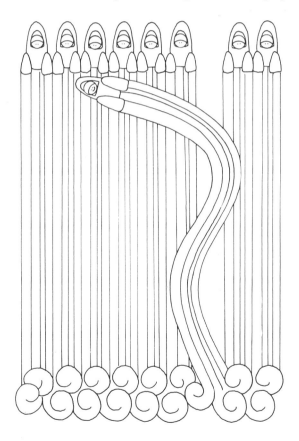

35

Blown-In
Cellulose Insulation

Get blown-in cellulose insulation. You've all heard of the advantages of insulation to enhance the energy efficiency of your home. However, usually you think of the rolls of pink colored fiberglass stuff rolled into an attic. The fact is that insulation and techniques for insulation may be more sophisticated than you realize.

For one thing, you no longer need to have your home insulated with only fiberglass insulation. There is another product called *cellulose insulation*, which is derived from recycled newspapers and sodium borate. This product, it so happens, is a more efficient insulator than fiberglass. As for installing insulation, particularly cellulose insulation, this material can be blown-in. In fact, cellulose insulation can be blown not only into your attic, but even behind your walls. To blow-in insulation means more surface area is covered with insulating material, which increases its insulating effectiveness.

Planet Saving Benefit:
Blown-in cellulose insulation is an advantage to us and our planet because it makes use of recycled newspapers and a planet-safe mineral, is easy to install, and makes your home more energy efficient.

Money Saving Benefit:
You can save up to 50% on your energy bills if your home has been insulated with cellulose insulation. Cellulose insulation may cost a few cents more per square foot (33¢ for cellulose versus 21¢ for fiberglass), but it will save you more money in the long run. For you technical buffs, cellulose has an R (insulating value) of 14; the fiberglass R value is only 9.

Where to Get it:

Call your local insulation contractor.
Check your telephone book under Insulation.

36

Caulking & Spackling

Get caulking and spackling compounds to seal up cracks around doors, windows, and holes in your walls. Insulation has been a proven means to save on energy. Even just a few holes and cracks here and there in your home can reduce energy efficiency by 10%. Why force your heating and cooling system to work harder? Taking the time is worth the effort, and it's easy.

Besides, these days you can get non-toxic and natural caulking and spackling compounds to seal up those cracks and holes.

Planet Saving Benefit:
Sealing up the holes and cracks in your house will reduce the amount of energy wasted. Energy: waste not, want not.

Money Saving Benefit:
Caulking and spackling compounds are a good investment in an effort to make your home more energy efficient. AFM caulking and spackling compounds are non-toxic and a fairly reasonable one-time investment. *AFM-24 Caulking Compound* is $8.60 per quart; *AFM-22 Spackling Compound* is $8.60 per quart. By caulking and spackling you can save up to 10% on your energy bill. A $100 monthly bill becomes a $90 bill. That's $120 per year in savings.

Where to Get it:
Caulking and spackling compounds are available at lumberyards and home improvement stores. However, we suggest you try compounds that won't harm you or our planet. Try non-toxic caulking and spackling compounds from AFM Enterprises. Contact them here:

AFM Enterprises, Inc.
1140 Stacy Court
Riverside, CA   92507
714/781-6860

37
Carpool/Vanpool

Get into a carpool or a vanpool. Split the expense for gas and maintenance, and you will find it definitely pays to carpool. How much can you save? Suppose you commute 10 miles to work and 10 miles back (that's 5 days per week). That's 4,800 miles of commuting per year give or take a few miles. Now suppose you have a car that gets 20 miles per gallon, and you buy regular unleaded gas and have a regular oil change. For all this you can expect to pay about $350 per year. If you spilt this expense (not including normal wear and tear) with one other person, that annual expense drops to $175. If you split with two other people, the expense is only $87.50 per year. Cutting your expenses by 50% or more is significant savings!

Besides saving money, you can also save time since many cities have special carpool lanes. On top of that, your nerves will be rewarded as well. When more than 30% of the time we spend driving is spent driving to work, it just makes sense to look for and get into a carpool.

Then there are vanpools. This is especially valuable for people who have a commute which exceeds an hour or more in one direction. Vanpools typically use 12 to 15 passenger vans (although mini-vans are also used). There are three types of vanpools: third party (commuters rent a van from a fleet management company, sharing the expense), employer-sponsored (such companies as 3M, Chevron, Northrop, and others do this), and owner-operated vanpools. For owner-operators, the owner buys the van, maintains it, pays for insurance, and charges a weekly or monthly fare to fellow commuters.

Planet Saving Benefit:
The emissions from cars are a major scourge of our planet. Smog, acid

rain, and global warming are just three major results of the fossil fuels our cars burn.

If we just consider smog, we find it is not only unhealthful to our bodies, but it also damages the foliage of forests, and according to the EPA has even reduced by 30% or more the capacity for some rural areas to produce crops. This is just the proverbial "tip of the iceberg."

Of course, if we don't curb our flagrant misuse of fossil fuels, and the bad results don't kill off people and the planet first, we may just run out of those precious fossil fuels. Some scientists forecast that at our current rate of consumption, we will run out of fossil fuels in the next 30 years.

Carpooling will cut down on the use of fossil fuels, and the emissions our cars release into the atmosphere. If commuters went to work in pairs, we could spare the use of more than 18 millions gallons of fuel. This also means more than 360 million pounds of greenhouse gas would not escape into the atmosphere.

Money Saving Benefit:
Getting into a carpool or vanpool is far cheaper than going solo. Also, you may be able to get a special car insurance break when you become a regular carpooler. Contact your insurance company. Owner-operator vanpoolers can get all the benefits of operating a business, including deducting all related expenses.

Where to Get it:
Find out about carpools at your work, or try to call a local carpool center. You may check in your telephone book under Carpools or Rideshare. To learn more about vanpooling, contact your county or state Department of Transportation for tips on programs and resources in your area.

38

Central Air Conditioning System

Get an efficient central air conditioning system. Central air conditioning systems, like heating systems, can be tremendous energy wasters. You can save on energy and money by avoiding use of your air conditioning whenever possible, perhaps when the temperature is not more than 78° F. Installing a fan-ventilation system in your attic can help draw hot air out, leaving cooler air behind. Also, try leaving windows open at night during cooler nighttime temperatures, and then shutting the windows in the morning to trap cool air. You may cut down your use of air conditioning by nearly half with these techniques alone.

However, if you happen to live in a very humid climate (like in this country's Deep South or New England), you may need air conditioning not only to cool the air, but to take out humidity in the air. Install the most energy efficient system you can buy. Check the Seasonal Energy Efficiency Rating (SEER). (Room air conditioners are measured in EERs.) The best type of central air conditioning system is rated at SEER 12 or above.

You can also get an energy saving attachment such as the *Conden Saver*. The *Conden Saver* uses the water runoff from your air conditioning system to cool the compressor coils of your system.

Planet Saving Benefit:

Avoiding the use of your air conditioner is the best way to cut down on the energy expended. Obviously, getting the most energy efficient system you can in the first place will save energy when you use your air conditioner. And when you can't get a new energy efficient system, attach a gizmo like the *Conden Saver* to make your existing air conditioning system operate more efficiently. All these efforts spell less energy consumed, and more energy available for the future.

Money Saving Benefit:

Adopting alternative practices to avoid using air conditioning will save you money, perhaps cutting your energy bill by as much as 50%. The Conden Saver can save you up to 30% on your cooling bill! Wow!

Where to Get it:

Get a Conden Saver for under $200. Conden Savers are available at this
source:

Kim Supply Company
1407 Kansas Ave.
Kansas City, MO   64127
800/444-2783

39

Clothesline

Get a clothesline. Dryers are not the biggest energy wasters of household appliances (consuming on average about 3% of the total energy in the house). But then, why waste energy when you don't have to?

A clothesline is an inexpensive, non-energy-wasting way to dry clothes. Besides, somehow, clothes dried on a line always seem a little fluffier and smell a little nicer. Try drying even *some* of your clothing on a clothesline, perhaps half of it.

Planet Saving Benefit:
Clotheslines are a clean, effective way to dry clothing without expending electric or fossil fuel energy. You also won't need to use fabric softeners. Everyone should try this to some extent.

Money Saving Benefit:
If you dry most of your clothes on a clothesline, your energy bill will be a little lower. Over time, such savings add up. But then, your initial cash outlay for such an investment is no great hardship anyway. Clotheslines cost $1 or $2.

Where to Get it:
You can either buy a clothesline, or make your own out of rope.

If you opt to buy one, you can get it at home improvement stores, supermarkets, and lumberyards.

40

Compressor

Get a new, high efficiency compressor for your central air conditioning system to replace your old compressor. The air conditioner compressor is that part of your central air conditioning system located outside of your home. The fact is that as your compressor ages, it becomes less and less energy efficient. And if your compressor is already about 10 or more years old, chances are your compressor is costing you more than it's worth. By just replacing your old compressor, with a more efficient, later model, you can save on energy and the money to cool your home.

Important point: make sure the new compressor is compatible with the unit inside your home. Otherwise, you won't save energy. A mismatched compressor can be as inefficient as an old one.

Planet Saving Benefit:
A new air compressor can substantially lower energy use by 20 to 50%. This is important when you consider that more than 60% of the homes in this country have air conditioning systems, and about 75% of new homes are being equipped with them.

Money Saving Benefit:
How much money you save by getting a new compressor versus keeping your old one depends on the age of your compressor. With a new and properly matched compressor, your system can be two times more efficient than your old one, which results in definite money savings.

How much it will cost to replace your old compressor depends on several criteria including the type of air conditioning unit model, the capacity of your unit, age of the unit, its location in your home, etc.

Where to Get it:
Get your new compressor from the air conditioning dealer who supplied you the old one. Your dealer can help you pick the right compressor to fit your particular air conditioning unit. Have your dealer look at your system to give you a price quote. Such a visit will cost you nothing.

41
Dishwasher

Get an energy- and water-efficient automatic dishwasher. Eighty percent of the energy consumed to operate your dishwasher is used to heat the water for washing your dishes. Dishwashers also swallow up to 14 gallons of water for each wash cycle. When buying a dishwasher, the trick is to find one that does not require a lot of water. This reduces water waste and the amount of energy needed to heat up all the water.

There are two types of dishwashers: compact and standard. Don't get a compact dishwasher. Why? Although a compact dishwasher may use less energy, it washes fewer dishes. You end up using this type of dishwasher more often, and expend more energy than necessary. Rather, get an energy efficient standard model. Features to look for include:

- *Booster heater.* This is a mechanism which boosts water heating. It makes it possible for you to lower the machine's thermostat, and save energy.

- *Energy-saving wash cycles.* If you have a light load, just set the wash cycle to "light." The machine doesn't work as hard, thus saving energy.

- *Energy-saving "no heat" dry.* When the "no heat" feature is selected, room air is circulated. The machine doesn't have to work. This saves energy.

The most energy efficient standard dishwasher on the market now is the A.E.G. Favorit 665i. Caloric and Modern Maid are also pretty good.

Planet Saving Benefit:
An efficient dishwasher saves water and energy. By just taking advantage of the wash cycle feature, you can nearly cut water consumption in half. This cuts down energy used. The booster heater alone can cut energy use by 5%.

Money Saving Benefit:
Investing in an energy efficient dishwasher will save you money. You save on your water bill, and you save on your energy bill. How much, of course, depends on if your previous dishwasher was an energy

spendthrift, or if you were just washing dishes by hand. You may find it hard to believe, but you may actually spend 37% more in water and energy doing dishes by hand. Something to consider for you diehard manual dishwashers.

Where to Get it:
Get dishwashers at major appliance stores, department stores, etc. Look in your phone book under Dishwashing Machine Dealers.

42

Double-Glazed Windows

Get double-glazed windows (or even single or triple-glazed windows) to increase the level of insulation in your home. Windows with a low insulating value (R-value), can waste about 1/3 of your home's energy for heating and cooling. Why? Because instead of retaining cool air when it's hot outside, or warm air when it's cold outside, a window with a low R-value lets air in and out of your home indiscriminately. This just forces your heating and cooling systems to work harder. The result: wasted energy.

To avoid wasting any more energy, install double-glazed windows. Double-glazed windows are windows specially designed for the purpose of enhancing insulating effectiveness.

Planet Saving Benefit:

Glazed windows can be as energy efficient as your insulated walls. This prevents the waste of energy, gas or electricity, depending on the type of heating/cooling system you use.

Money Saving Benefit:

Double-glazed windows are not cheap, costing as much as $200 to $400 per window, depending on size. But they are an investment that will pay off over time. Upon installing these windows throughout your home, you will see immediate energy savings. In fact, depending on the number of windows you have in your home, and the climate, you could save more than 20% of your energy bill with energy efficient windows.

Where to Get it:

Double-glazed windows, as well as windows with a sandwiched layer of insulating gases like argon or krypton, are available at department stores and window dealers.

Check your telephone book.

43
Dryer Exhaust Vent Hood

Get a dryer exhaust vent hood. A dryer exhaust who? Dryers are often installed in such a way that they vent to the outside of your home. Now, many people don't realize that if the vent outside does not have a hood, cold air can creep into the house, forcing your heating system to work harder. But you may think that the little flap covering your dryer vent is good enough. That's not true, since the little flap is not tight fitting and outside air gets in anyway. In effect, you have a hole in your wall to the outside. To avoid wasting more energy, get a tight fitting vent hood.

Planet Saving Benefit:
Installing a dryer vent hood is like caulking and insulating your house. When you keep the outside air out, you don't put an unnecessary strain on your heating and cooling system. This saves energy. This also reduces the amount of carbon dioxide released into the atmosphere from your heating and cooling system.

Money Saving Benefit:
Getting a tight-sealing dryer vent hood is not a huge investment at only $2 to $4. Consider that it is in the same category as caulking, spackling, and insulation. Just one more good way to cut energy costs expended for heating and cooling your house.

Where to Get it:
Get a dryer vent hood from the same place you got your dryer. Otherwise, you can try your local home improvement store (the warehouse variety). One brand to look for is made by Deflecto Corp. Deflecto can be contacted here:

Deflecto Corp.
P.O. Box 50057
Indianapolis, IN 46250
317/849-9555

44

Compact Fluorescent Light Bulbs

Get compact fluorescent light bulbs in place of your common incandescent light bulbs.

Planet Saving Benefit:

Incandescent light bulbs are huge energy wasters. They convert to light only about 10% of the energy they use. This is very wasteful when you consider that 25% of all electricity consumed in the U.S. is consumed by inefficient lights. Besides this, up to 10% of your energy bill can be consumed by lighting.

The answer to this dilemma: we should use energy efficient compact fluorescent light bulbs. They use up to 75% less energy than incandescents and can last up to 12 times longer!

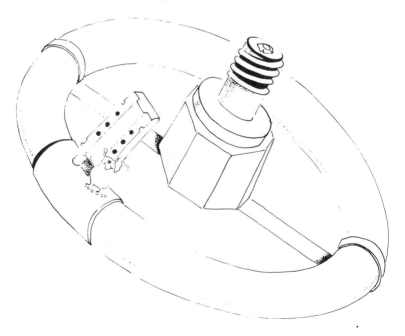

Fluorescent light bulbs are usually not spherical in shape like regular, incandescent light bulbs. They are either round, or consist of tubes bent to look like the letter "U." Despite the odd shapes of fluorescents, they are designed to fit in most conventional incandescent light fixtures.

Saving energy is important, especially in this country. Americans are the greatest energy wasters in the world. With only 5% of the world population, we squander about 25% of the world's energy resources. Changing to fluorescent light bulbs is the least we can do (although we should and can do much more).

Money Saving Benefit:
Compact fluorescents use less energy and are cooler (which saves on air-conditioning costs). The total energy costs for 9,000 hours of light from a compact fluorescent is $11, versus $49.75 for the same number of hours from an incandescent bulb. Fluorescents start from $11 on up. However, prices are dropping because of the increased popularity of these bulbs. Always shop around. For now, the initial investment may turn some people off a little, but the benefits become clear in the long run.

Where to Get it:
Get compact fluorescent light bulbs from ecology stores, and lighting stores (you may need to try a commercial store), home improvement stores, or order by mail. The fact is, nearly all the major light bulb manufacturers now produce compact fluorescent light bulbs. There is no reason why you cannot ask your local grocery store manager to order and stock compact fluorescent light bulbs in his store. In fact, the more people who do this, the faster the prices will drop. In the meantime, here is one mail order source:

The New Alchemy Institute
237 Hatchville Road
East Falmouth, MA   02536
508/564-6301

45
Electronic Ballasts

Get an electronic ballast for your tube fluorescent lamp. You may not be aware that fluorescent lights provide more light than any other source, except for the sun of course. In fact, tube fluorescent lamps annually burn up the energy equivalent of 30 large power plants! That's amazing. Therefore, if you can't or don't want to just get rid of your tube fluorescent lamp, anything to make these lights more energy efficient is smart. One way to do this is to install electronic ballasts into your fluorescent fixtures. They reduce energy used and even eliminate the annoying hum or flicker of tube fluorescent lamps.

Planet Saving Benefit:
Installing electronic ballasts in your fluorescent fixtures will reduce the electricity consumed by those fixtures by as much as 40 to 50%!

Money Saving Benefit:
Anything you can get to cut your energy as dramatically as an electronic ballast is a good investment. Save up to 50% on your lighting electric bill if your light source is exclusively fluorescent. This is especially good for businesses. Electronic ballasts cost anywhere from $38 to $75 depending on the type of fluorescent fixtures you have.

Where to Get it:
Get electronic ballasts from home improvement centers or commercial lighting stores. You can also try this source:

Electronic Ballast Technology
2510 West 237 St.
Suite 102
Torrance, CA   90505
800/654-6501

Electronic Ballast Technology claims to be the largest, exclusive electronic ballast maker in the world.

46
Enro Heatsaver

Get an Enro Heatsaver to install in your water heater. An Enro What? Most conventional water heaters are not very energy efficient. The Enro Heatsaver is the only system of its kind that uses the waste heat from your central air conditioning system to heat the water in your water heater. In fact, during the summer, you can disconnect the heater of your water heater, and the Enro Heatsaver system will heat your water. Meanwhile, your air conditioner will operate more efficiently.

Planet Saving Benefit:
The Enro Heatsaver is an excellent energy saver because it makes both your water heater and your air conditioning system more efficient. Saving energy is always a step in the right direction.

Money Saving Benefit:
For the benefit this system yields, the Enro Heatsaver is a great investment. Especially when you consider that an Enro Heatsaver is only $174. And what can make this system even more inviting is that many utility companies offer rebates to people who install the Enro Heatsaver. In Texas, for example, you can get a $100 rebate.

Another good thing is that you can install this system yourself. It is estimated that you could save up to 20% or more on your energy bills with this system.

Note: You may want to check your water heater warranty to make sure such a modification won't violate the warranty. Unless, of course, you don't care.

Where to Get it:
It is best to get the Enro Heatsaver directly from the manufacturer (it's cheaper that way). Contact this source:

Enro Manufacturing
6461 Garden Road
Riviera Beach, FL 33404
407/845-0465

47
Faucet Aerator

Usable water is getting scarcer every day. Of all the water on earth, only 1% is available to us to drink. Of this 1%, one part comes from streams, rivers, and lakes, and the rest comes from underground sources. Unfortunately, a growing percentage of our drinkable water is becoming undrinkable - thanks to toxic waste disposal.

So, to help conserve water, get a faucet aerator and dramatically reduce the volume of water you use every day, perhaps by as much as 50%. A faucet aerator is a clever device that reduces the flow of water, but aerates the water to cause it to flow with greater force!

Planet Saving Benefit:
If we all installed faucet aerators, Americans could save more than 91 billion gallons of water per year!

Money Saving Benefit:
Cut your water consumption in half, and cut your water and drainage bill in half. At the very least, even if you don't cut your bill in half, you can see that some savings is possible.

Where to Get it:
A faucet aerator costs under $10 and can be purchased at home improvement stores or you can order by mail. One source is:

Rising Sun Enterprises
Box 586
Old Snowmass, CO 81654
303/927-8051

48
Gas Appliances

Get energy efficient gas appliances. Gas appliances are about 50% more energy efficient than electrical appliances. This means such high energy consuming devices as washers and dryers, stoves, dishwashers, etc., which run on electricity, can be replaced by less wasteful gas appliances.

Now, if you can't afford (or it is simply not practical) to replace your electrical appliances, at least try to refrain from using them during peak, daytime hours. Instead, use them at night (e.g., wash your clothes only at night).

Planet Saving Benefit:
If we get gas appliances, we can conserve electrical energy used. And this is smart because electrical energy is often derived from such sources as nuclear power plants. The New England states draw 1/3 of their electricity from nuclear energy. Most states rely on nuclear energy to some extent. In fact, 38 states have one or more nuclear power plants. Illinois has 13 of them.

The problem with nuclear power is that there is always a threat of radioactive leaks, like at Three-Mile Island in 1979. In 1987 there were 341 automatic shut downs, although shut downs are fewer than before.

The other problem with nuclear power plants is what to do about the dangerous, radioactive nuclear waste. Several nuclear power plants can't contain their waste, and 73 plants will reach capacity before the year 2000. Moreover, there is concern over the effectiveness of the existing nuclear waste storage technology. Obviously, the less we rely on electricity, the less many of us have to rely on such potentially hazardous energy sources.

Money Saving Benefit:
We save money with gas appliances over electrical appliances. So, looking into gas appliances is a good idea when we are in the market to replace our more costly electrical appliances. Check the energy efficiency rating posted with yellow stickers on each appliance.

Where to Get it:
Gas appliances are available at all major department stores (Sears Roebuck has a good selection), or appliance retail shops.

49
Gasket Insulators

Get gasket insulators to insulate behind wall outlets and switches. Believe it or not, you actually waste energy by allowing your wall outlets and wall switches to serve as openings in your walls. So, when you try to heat, the warm air escapes through these openings, and cold air comes in; when you try to cool, cool air escapes and hot air gets in. This is one of those hidden energy wasters most people never think of. The answer to this dilemma is: gasket insulators.

A gasket insulator is simply a foam device that you install behind your wall outlets and wall switches to make them air-tight.

Planet Saving Benefit:

Use gasket insulators to close up those openings in your wall and save perhaps more than 10% on energy. The rule of thumb: less energy wasted, the more energy we'll have later on.

Money Saving Benefit:

When you save on energy, you save on money. Gasket insulators are cheap and easy to install. They are clearly a good one-time investment. Gasket insulators cost about $3 for a packet of 12.

Where to Get it:

Get gasket insulators at most lumberyards
or home improvement stores.

50
Halogen Lighting

Get halogen or tungsten-halogen lighting for precise light focusing. Compact fluorescents are probably the most efficient type of light you could use to light rooms and for other common lighting applications. However, if you need very precise, quality light focused in a particular area, like for working or possibly reading, halogen or tungsten-halogen lights are actually more energy efficient than compact fluorescents.

It so happens that the energy efficiency of halogen lights has been improved in the last few years. And if you install these lights in reflector type fixtures, they are even more efficient.

Planet Saving Benefit:
Cutting down the energy we use to light up our homes is good for our planet. Halogen lights, if applied appropriately, can help out in our effort to save energy. Apparently, for precise lighting, halogens are up to 40% more energy efficient than compact fluorescents.

Money Saving Benefit:
If you use halogen lights for precise lighting, combined with compact fluorescent lights for lighting the rest of your home, you can save even more money on electricity than without the halogen lights. Halogens and tungsten-halogens are usually a little cheaper than compact fluorescents. A halogen light for reading could cost about $4 for a 50 watt bulb and will last 2,400 hours (more than 3 times longer than a 50 watt incandescent).

Where to Get it:
Sylvania and General Electric manufacture some excellent halogen lights intended as replacements for incandescent lights. You can get these lights at many supermarkets, hardware stores, and light stores. Halogen lights intended for halogen fixtures are available at light stores (retail and commercial). Or you can try this mail order source:

People's Energy Resource Cooperative
354 Waverly Street
Framingham, MA 01701
508/879-8572

51
Heating System Tune-Up

Get a heating system tune-up. You have heard of a tune-up for your car, but you may not have heard of a tune-up for your heating system. The fact is, if you own an oil-fueled or a gas-fueled heating system, you should have your heating system tuned up regularly. Otherwise, you are probably wasting energy.

Oil systems should be tuned up once per year. Gas systems should be tuned up at least once every two years.

The technician will test, tune, and clean your heating system as necessary. Such things as the burner, the combustion chamber, heat exchanger surfaces, oil line filter, and flue pipe must be cleaned.

Planet Saving Benefit:
An oil or gas fueled heating system that gets a regular tune-up will operate more energy efficiently. We must all make an effort to save our planet's unreplenishable fossil fuels. Also, an efficient heating system will not contribute more carbon dioxide into the atmosphere.

Money Saving Benefit:
A regular tune-up of your heating system can save you up to 10% on your heating bill. This makes the $40 to $60 cost for the tune up a good investment. By the way, a regular tune-up of your heating system will also increase its lifespan.

Where to Get it:

To get a tune-up, call your utility company. Otherwise, look up Heating Contractors in the telephone book.

52
Heat-Pump Heating System

Get a heat-pump heating system. This is especially appropriate for people with electric furnaces or electric resistance heat. Also, you can benefit from a heat pump in new housing, in areas with moderate climate where the gas and electric companies are competing against eachother with high efficiency equipment. Remember: an inefficient heating system in your home does two things that are harmful to our planet:

- Wastes energy
- Releases carbon dioxide into the atmosphere.

If you have an inefficient heating system (like one which relies on electricity), you may be burning up half the energy just to keep the thing running. This is a waste. And the carbon dioxide released just adds to the carbon dioxide gas accumulated over our planet and is heating up the planet (commonly known as the greenhouse effect).

The heat pump takes advantage of thermal energy from outside air. Heat pumps make efficient cooling systems, too!

Planet Saving Benefit:
The less energy you waste for heating, the more energy we have left. Plus, a more efficient heating system prevents further accumulation of greenhouse gases.

Money Saving Benefit:
A heat pump can cost about $2,000 for most homes, and the price goes up from there. This is no small change. But you will see a dramatic drop in your heating bill, perhaps as much as 60%!

Where to Get it:
Get your heat pump from Lennox Heating & Cooling Systems.

Check your telephone book for the nearest
Lennox dealer in your city.

53
Heat Traps

Get heat traps if your water heater did not come equipped with them. A hot water heater without heat traps or one-way valves means that as hot water rises and cold water falls within the hot and cold water pipes, the heat from the hot water heater escapes through the pipes. This wastes energy used for heating the water. However, heat traps installed on both the hot and cold water pipes will reduce the amount of heat that escapes from these pipes.

To ensure greater energy efficiency, whether or not your hot water heater has heat traps, make the added investment of wrapping insulation around your water pipes near the water heater.

Planet Saving Benefit:
Heat traps and insulated pipes near your water heater will reduce the amount of energy which would otherwise be wasted. Also, if water in pipes is hot, you won't run water at the tap so long waiting for water to heat up, and you'll save water.

Money Saving Benefit:
Heat traps are not expensive: about $30. They are an investment you make once, and will pay back from then on up to $30 per year.

Where to Get it:
Get your heat traps from hardware stores, home improvement stores, or your local water heater dealer.

54

Home Energy Audit

Get a home energy audit. You may not feel qualified or adequately informed about how to diagnose ways to improve the energy efficiency of your home. Of course, reading this book will help you get acquainted with things you can get to make your home more efficient; however, you *can* consult an expert.

There are home energy consultants who can conduct an energy audit of your home and make recommendations on how you can save energy and save money. Often these consultants can even direct you to various sources in your area to get the things you need to make your home more energy efficient. Ten years ago there were very few of these consultants. Fortunately, along with the growing concern about the state of our planet, more and more of these consultants are now available.

Planet Saving Benefit:
A home energy consultant can find things in your home that you would not even think of. If you follow the advice of these consultants, you will reduce the amount of energy you use in your home. It's that simple.

Money Saving Benefit:
A more energy efficient home is a home that will not cost as much to run in contrast to a home that wastes energy. The home energy audit and the recommendations of an informed energy consultant can be a smart investment. In fact, very often, such consultation can be conducted by your utility company for a nominal charge and may be free (particularly if you're a senior citizen). Or you can hire an energy consultant for around $50 to $100.

Where to Get it:
To get a home energy audit, call your local utility company. Find out if they do energy audits, and if they cost anything. Otherwise, look in the phone book under Energy, Energy Management, or Conservation Consultants.

55
Low-Flow Shower Head

Get a low-flow shower head. About 30% of the water used in our households is used for taking showers and baths. Obviously, this is a significant drain on our limited usable water supply. Additionally, the energy consumed to heat that shower and bath water is second only to heating and cooling our homes: up to 30% of the energy bill!

Fortunately, we can curb unnecessary waste of water and energy to heat water simply by installing a low-flow shower head. The low-flow shower head can cut water flow by up to 80% without sacrificing the force of the water flow. And since less water flows through the head, less of it needs to be heated.

Furthermore, when you get your low-flow shower head, avoid taking baths; on average, baths use twice as much water and energy as showers.

Planet Saving Benefit:
By using a low-flow shower head we conserve both water and the energy to heat the water. The more of us that do this, the better.

Money Saving Benefit:
The less water and energy you use for showers, the more money you will save. And sometimes a low-flow shower head will cost you nothing: you can't lose! However, if you do have to buy one, they cost no more than $10.

Where to Get it:
You may be able to get a free low-flow shower head from your utility company. Give them a call. Otherwise, you can probably pick one up at your local home improvement store (the warehouse variety), or just mail order one. Here is one source:

Water Conservation Systems
Damonmill Square
Concord, MA   01742
800/462-3341

56
Low-Flush Toilet

Get a low-flush toilet. Toilets can waste a great deal of water. Most toilets will flush up to 8 gallons of water, when only about 2 or 3 are really necessary. Toilet dams are effective water conservation means, but you could also just get a low-flush toilet. A low-flush toilet is just a toilet designed to use no more than up to 3 gallons of water per flush. Some low-flush toilets will even operate on less than a gallon of water per flush.

Planet Saving Benefit
With a low-flush toilet, you will not waste as much water as with a conventional toilet. We desperately need to conserve water, and this is one good way to do that.

Money Saving Benefit:
Low-flush toilets are not expensive, and will quickly pay for themselves. The *Peerless Water Saver* low-flush toilet uses only 1.6 gallons of water to flush, and costs only $43. This is one of the cheaper, more efficient low-flush toilets on the market.

Where to Get it:
You can probably get a *Peerless Water Saver* low-flush toilet or a comparable toilet at many home improvement stores (the warehouse variety). You can also contact the company that makes the *Peerless Water Saver* at this source:

Peerless Pottery, Inc.
North Lincoln Ave., P.O. Box 145
Rockport, IN 47635
812/649-2261

You can get further information about low-flush toilets, and prices to purchase by mail order, from this source:

Resource Conservation Technology
2633 North Calvert St.
Baltimore, MD 21218
301/366-1146

57
Microwave Oven

Get a microwave oven. Conventional cook-top stoves, which include the common kitchen range, are not always the most energy efficient or cost effective. This is especially true when cooking small quantities of food.

Planet Saving Benefit:

Microwave ovens are a good way to reduce the amount of energy we use to cook our food. And if you're worried about the safeness of using a microwave, these days they are usually well built and leak proof.

Also, when you use a microwave, you reduce the amount of carbon dioxide dumped into the atmosphere as the result of cooking. In the case of the conventional oven mentioned in the example below, the energy used to cook a casserole would result in dumping 4 pounds of carbon dioxide into the atmosphere. The microwave oven, of course, would release much less carbon dioxide into the atmosphere.

Money Saving Benefit:

Microwave ovens use less than 20% the energy it takes for conventional ovens to cook. Over time, the money adds up. And these days, microwave oven prices are dropping. You can easily find a good one for under $150. They also last forever, as long as you care for them.

As an example of cost savings, to cook a casserole in your conventional oven would take 1 hour at 350° F and cost 16¢. Not only that, but your oven would expend about 2 kWh of energy. Now, if you get a microwave oven, you can cook that casserole in 15 minutes, which costs you only 3¢, and you would expend only .36 kWh of energy.

Where to Get it:

Get a microwave oven at most kitchen appliance stores, department stores, and various specialty shops.

Check your telephone book.

58
Modulating Aquastat

Get a modulating aquastat for your hot water fueled heating system. If you have a hot water boiler heating system, chances are that your boiler maintains its temperature at around 180° F before circulating the water to radiators and baseboards. This may be fine for cold weather, but is totally wasteful during warmer months. To control the temperature in the boiler, so that it reaches higher temperatures during colder weather, and drops its temperature during warmer weather, use a modulating aquastat.

A modulating aquastat is a device that senses weather changes and raises or lowers the temperature accordingly.

Planet Saving Benefit:
A modulating aquastat is another ingenious invention that can save energy. Energy-saving inventions are among the best type of inventions to know about and to use.

Money Saving Benefit:
You can save up to 15% on your fuel bill by installing a modulating aquastat. The most noted brand names for modulating aquastats include Enertrol™ and Mastermind™. They cost between $150 and $350.

Where to Get it:
Get your modulating aquastat through your local heating contractor. Ask for the brand names mentioned above.

59
Occupancy Sensor

Get an occupancy sensor in each room of your home. Most people have trouble remembering to turn off lights when they leave a room. The result: wasted energy in the form of a light that is on and doesn't need to be on. Answer: an occupancy sensor.

An occupancy sensor is a device that is connected to your light; it turns your light on when it senses the heat of your body or your movement in the room.

Planet Saving Benefit:
Occupancy sensors help save energy and that's a good thing. Lights only come on when they need to be on. Any other time, they're off. What a great idea!

Money Saving Benefit:
If you have a tendency to just let your lights burn all by themselves, you need to make this investment. They cost about $20 to $40 each. Consider this as another one of those one-time investments. You buy it once, and forget about it. In the meantime, you do something to save our planet and save money at the same time.

Where to Get it:
Getting an occupancy sensor may require going through mail order. However, there is a growing demand for these devices apart from commercial users, and this means retailers will stock them. Here's one source to contact:

Intermatic
Intermatic Plaza
Spring Grove, IL   60081
815/675-2321

60
Power Burner

Get a power burner for your gas heating system. Many people have old coal or oil heating systems in their homes that have been converted to run on gas. But even this conversion is not necessarily the most energy efficient way to go. To make your system more efficient, you need to get a high efficiency gas power burner to replace the burner on your furnace or boiler.

Power burners regulate the air entering the burner of your heating system. If your system receives too little air, this can be dangerous. If your system receives too much air, this can yield inefficient combustion. Have a technician check out your system to determine if it has been equipped with a power burner.

Planet Saving Benefit:
A power burner installed in your gas heating system is a good way to save energy. Not only that, but the less we waste for heating, the fewer carbon gases we'll be dumping into the atmosphere.

Money Saving Benefit:
A power burner can cut your fuel bill by up to 20%. That's big savings! Of course, the cost for a power burner is not exactly cheap at around $500. But you may see this system pay for itself in perhaps as little as 2 years.

Where to Get it:
Get a power burner through your local heating contractor. However, before you get the power burner, have the heating contractor come out to determine if you need one.

Chances are this initial visit will cost you nothing.

61
Programmable Clock Thermostat

Get a programmable clock thermostat. Having control over our heating can be a challenge. First, if we don't begin with an efficient heating system, we are wasting all sorts of energy just keeping that system in operation. But even if we have an efficient heating system, we may still be wasting energy. How? By not regulating the level of heating throughout the day and night.

The fact is that there are certain times during the day when you require a higher level of heating than other times of the day. If you just keep the system blasting without regard to varying heating levels, you're going to waste energy. Answer: get a programmable clock thermostat. This is a computerized gadget to use in place of the conventional thermostat. With the programmable clock thermostat you can program to raise and lower your heating for specific times during the day.

Planet Saving Benefit:
If you get a programmable clock thermostat, and program it to reduce temperatures at night and during times when you're away, and then have the temperature rise when you need it, you can save up to 40% of the energy used! Oh yes, having a system that operates more efficiently also reduces the amount of carbon dioxide released into the atmosphere.

Money Saving Benefit:
A programmable clock thermostat will cost around $50 to $100. When you consider that you will save 15 to 40% of the energy you use for heating, it's not a bad investment. In fact, your investment will probably be paid back in about a year.

Where to Get it:
You can get a programmable clock thermostat at department stores, some appliance shops, and from a heating and cooling system dealer.

Check your telephone book.

62
Radiator Vent

Get an adjustable radiator vent or valve. Some people have radiators in their homes for heating. These are not always energy efficient because the valves to regulate heat flow can be turned down, but not turned off in a room where heat is not needed. To remedy this, and make your radiator more energy efficient, you can get an adjustable air vent. The adjustable air vent will enable you to completely turn on or turn off your radiator heat flow.

If you happen to have a steam radiator, you can achieve greater control over heat flow by installing a thermostatic radiator valve. This device enables you to set the temperature for each room, and the radiator will heat until it reaches that temperature, and then be turned off by the thermostatic radiator valve.

Planet Saving Benefit:
Radiator vents and valves make it possible to keep energy usage manageable. Less energy wasted, more energy available. It's that simple.

Money Saving Benefit:
An adjustable radiator vent is a small investment of about $10 to $15. And it is not hard to install. You just unscrew the old vent, and screw on the new one. A small investment, but one that can dramatically improve energy efficiency and save you money.

Thermostatic radiators cost somewhat more, ranging about $50 to $150. But buying one is far cheaper than hiring someone to reinstall your home's piping. Besides, you will save money on utilities with these devices installed.

Where to Get it:
Get radiator vents and valves from most hardware
and heating supply stores.

63
Refrigerator

Get an energy efficient refrigerator. The refrigerator is the greatest home appliance energy hog. If possible, we should try to buy the refrigerator that has been rated as the most energy efficient according to what we can afford.

Currently, the most energy efficient refrigerator on the market is the Sun Frost refrigerator. This refrigerator is reported to reduce the amount of energy consumed by up to 80% of the energy that a refrigerator would normally consume.

There are several simple energy and money saving tips you can adopt. For example, make sure you never locate your refrigerator next to your stove, dishwasher, or even next to a window that lets in a lot of sun. A refrigerator next to a hot appliance or a sunny window has to work harder to cool. Also, give your refrigerator at least 1 inch of breathing space all around it. This gives it sufficient air-circulation to make it operate efficiently.

Another good idea is to just make sure the temperature in your refrigerator is set properly for maximum energy efficiency. The main refrigerator compartment should be set between 36° to 38° F.

The freezer compartment should be set at between 0° to 5° F.

Planet Saving Benefit:
If we use refrigerators which are more energy efficient, we will use less energy. And we Americans waste far too much energy.

Money Saving Benefit:
An energy efficient refrigerator means lower energy bills. For example, if you were to buy the Sun Frost refrigerator, you would reduce your overall average monthly energy bill by 10%. The Sun Frost refrigerator is not cheap: $2,500. Other very efficient refrigerators are less than half this cost, depending on size and features.

When buying appliances, just check the energy rating sticker (usually colored yellow) on the appliance and compare it with other similar appliances.

Where to Get it:
You can get energy efficient appliances in most department stores and appliance shops. If you are interested in the Sun Frost refrigerator, here's the address:

Sun Frost
P.O. Box 1101
Arcata, CA   95521
707/822-9095

64

Refrigerator Brush

Get a refrigerator brush. Say what? Yes. A refrigerator brush.

Refrigerators use up about 10% or more of your total energy bill. As we mentioned before, they are the most energy consuming appliance in your home. Some refrigerators are more energy efficient than others. However, regardless of the make or model of your refrigerator, the refrigerator coils (located either underneath or behind your refrigerator) can get clogged with dirt and debris. Usually, homeowners let these coils get clogged; the refrigerator works harder (consuming more energy) and eventually fails. This often leads to expensive service calls, or possibly the need to replace the refrigerator.

One simple way to clean these coils is to use a specially designed refrigerator brush. The brush comes with a long handle and has tough hog's hair bristles. This brush can easily remove anything that has built up on your refrigerator coils.

Planet Saving Benefit:
If we all got a refrigerator brush and kept our coils clean, our refrigerators would operate about 10% more efficiently. Which means they would not be using up as much energy.

Money Saving Benefit:
A refrigerator with clean coils will not use as much energy as one with dirty coils. Also, such a refrigerator will last longer, and will avoid expensive service calls. For $6.95, such a brush is a good investment.

Where to Get it:
Get your refrigerator brush from this source:

Seventh Generation
49 Hercules Drive
Colchester, VT   05446
800/456-1177

65
Refrigerator Door Seal

Get a new refrigerator door seal or gasket to replace an old, worn, inefficient door seal or gasket. The rubber-like seal or gasket of your refrigerator door can have a lot to do with whether or not your refrigerator operates at optimum energy efficiency. And since the refrigerator is the most energy consuming appliance in your home, it's something worth investigating.

To check if your seal works efficiently, you can do one of a couple of things:

• Put a dollar bill in the door and close the door. If it falls, you need a new seal.

• The dollar test won't work if you have a magnetic door seal. Instead, put a 150-watt flood lamp inside your refrigerator. Direct the light toward a part of the seal. In a dim light, if light shines though, you need a new seal. (Check the bottom of the seal with a mirror.)

Planet Saving Benefit:
Up to 10% of your household energy is spent on keeping your refrigerator operating. A well-sealed refrigerator will prevent an increase in the percentage of energy used. A new seal could actually reduce the amount of energy used for refrigeration.

Money Saving Benefit:
Replacing a worn seal can help reduce your refrigeration costs. Replacing an old door seal can cost between $75 and $150 dollars for parts and labor. The door seal itself costs $35 to $75 (depending on make and model), but it takes an expert to install it. With a new door seal you will immediately notice that your refrigerator operates more efficiently, and this will reflect in a little less in energy expense.

Where to Get it:
Should you decide to replace your old seal with a new one, go back to your original refrigerator or appliance dealer. Or check in your phone book under Refrigerator Equipment - Supplies & Parts - Whol.

66
Solar Powered Flashlight

Get a solar powered flashlight. Solar powered flashlight? Yes. Believe it or not, they exist. Everyone needs a flashlight sooner or later. You never know when there will be a power failure (unless you operate on solar panels, obviously), or some other emergency or whatever, that calls for a flashlight. Why not use one that operates on solar energy?

Jade Mountain puts out a solar powered flashlight. Now, although their flashlight must have a rechargeable battery to operate, that's no problem if you install Millennium™ batteries as suggested earlier in this book. The flashlight soaks up the sun, converts that light to energy, and feeds it to the batteries, which retain that energy until you use the flashlight. It's entirely conceivable that you may *never* have to replace the batteries (or the flashlight).

Planet Saving Benefit:
A solar powered flashlight is another good example of how we can harness an energy source that does not exploit our planet. More of us should look into alternative energy sources when possible. The fact is solar energy is not only feasible, but there are a number of useful products available that take advantage of this free, clean energy source.

Money Saving Benefit:
Assuming for a moment that this is a once-in-a-lifetime investment, the price for the Jade Mountain solar powered flashlight is not that bad. In fact, you can keep it until you pass on, and then it can be passed on as an heirloom. How much is it? One flashlight is $32.

Where to Get it:
Get your solar powered flashlight and more information about solar energy and solar power from this source:

Jade Mountain
P.O. Box 4616
Boulder, CO   80306
303/449-6601

67

Space Heater

Get a space heater for localized home heating. It's always good to get a tip on learning how to keep warm in the winter while saving energy and money at the same time. Most of you have some type of heating system designed to heat your entire home. And there are ways to make such a system more efficient (as indicated elsewhere in this book). But you might consider the space heater as an additional means of heating.

The space heater is usually a small, box-like, electric gadget with heating elements intended to be used for heating small areas in your home. Other safer and more efficient space heaters (albeit, more costly) are space heaters fueled with natural gas that vent to the outside of your home.

The fact is you could very well lower the thermostat of your main heating system, and use your space heater to warm up only the room you plan to occupy most of the time. However, it is not advisable to attempt to heat an entire home with space heaters; this is neither energy efficient nor is it particularly safe (depending on the circumstances, and the heater, a space heater left unattended may start a fire).

Planet Saving Benefit:
If you employ selective heating with a space heater, you can reduce the amount of energy needed to heat your entire home. This cuts down on the use of either electric or fossil fuel energy sources.

Money Saving Benefit:
Space heaters start at about $30 and go up. There are no moving parts, so nothing wears very much over time. Therefore, these are an investment which you could have for many years of selective heating. Also, if you use the space heater enough, you could see a difference in your heating bill.

Where to Get it:
Space heaters are available at department stores, appliance shops, at heating and cooling dealers, and (believe it or not) a number of pharmacies.

68

Squeeze Nozzle

Get a squeeze nozzle for your garden hose. Apparently, Americans are compulsive lawn and garden waterers. You love to stand out there and water the vegetation. In fact, so much so that every week you over-water lawns and gardens by up to 216 billion gallons of water.

One way to restrict water use is to get a squeeze nozzle for the garden hose. This nozzle is designed to restrict the amount of water that sprays out of the hose. Then water infrequently, letting the grass get dry between waterings. Also, to avoid water evaporation, water in the evening rather than in the middle of the day.

Planet Saving Benefit:
If you get a squeeze nozzle for your garden hose, and adopt a few simple watering tips, you may actually break your compulsive water wasting habit. It takes will power! The result: you'll have water left to water your lawns and gardens in the future.

Money Saving Benefit:
Using less water for watering means you save money. If you cut down, or actually eliminate further water wasting, you may reduce your lawn and garden watering expense by 20 to 40%. A squeeze nozzle should cost about $5.

Where to Get it:
Get your squeeze nozzle at your local nursery store, lumberyard, home improvement store, or department store.

69

Tankless Water Heater

Get a tankless water heater (especially if you have a small household - up to two adults). Water heaters use up a large percentage of the energy used in your home (up to 31%). And your conventional water heater keeps a tank of water hot all the time, whether or not you use the hot water. This is not only unnecessary, but wastes energy. One alternative is to get a highly efficient tankless water heater designed to cut energy by not storing water, and heating water only when it is needed. (However, if you live in a hot climate, such as in Arizona, a tankless hot water heater may not be necessary since incoming water is usually already pretty warm.)

What does it look like? The tankless water heater looks very much like your conventional water heater only smaller, and can be located in the same place you would put a conventional water heater. The reason it can produce instant hot water throughout your entire home is that it has a series of coils which immediately heat up water contained in them. This coil and heat system is so efficient that hot water can flow through continuously if necessary.

Planet Saving Benefit:
Tankless water heaters are an excellent way to reduce energy use for water heating. They are also a good way to save on the water you normally run, while waiting for the water to get hot.

Money Saving Benefit:
You can save up to 50% on your energy costs for water heating with a tankless water heater. A tankless water heater starts at $100 and goes up, depending on the water and BTU capacity. They are a good investment; on average, this type of water heater pays for itself within 2 years.

Where to Get it:
Get your tankless water heater through your local water heater dealer. We recommend you check out *Paloma* and *Aqua Star* tankless water heaters. Consult your phone book. You can also try this source:

Real Goods Trading Co.
3041 Guidiville Rd.
Ukiah, CA   95482
800/688-9288

70
Television

Get rid of your television, or at least unplug it when not in use. Your T.V. actually draws electrical energy even when it's turned off. In fact, your T.V. contributes to the 6% of electricity used by your small electrical appliances (i.e., toasters, waffle makers, blenders, crock pots, etc.).

Remembering to unplug your T.V. may take some time as you develop such an energy-conserving habit. But considering that so little is worth watching on the idiot box these days, you may just opt to get rid of your television. And if you choose to take such a drastic measure, don't just throw your T.V. out, but give it away, perhaps to a charitable group or some couch potatoes you happen to know.

Planet Saving Benefit:
Unplugging your T.V. saves energy. Never getting a T.V. in the first place saves the energy which a T.V. would ultimately require during its use, and reduces the amount of raw materials and energy it takes to manufacture a new T.V.

Money Saving Benefit:
Giving away your television not only saves you the cost of using it, and any repair costs that you may incur during the life of the T.V., but you can make it a tax deductible contribution if you give it to a non-profit charitable organization. Again, if you need to keep your boob tube, at least unplug the thing when it's not in use.

71
Toilet Dam

Get a water conserving toilet dam. Toilets do not need the 5 to 8 gallons of water the typical toilet uses to flush. In fact, your conventional toilet can flush very nicely with only 2 to 3 gallons. Anything more than that is just a waste of water. The way to cut down the use of water in your toilet is to put a toilet dam in your toilet tank.

A toilet dam is simply a barrier, a "dam," that displaces water in the tank so the toilet flushes with less water.

Planet Saving Benefit:
If we install toilet dams in our toilets, our toilets don't use as much water. Using a toilet dam could save up to 12,000 gallons per year in a family of four.

Money Saving Benefit:
If your toilet uses less water, you can save money on your water bill. A toilet dam is no big investment at about $7 per set of dams for one toilet. However, you can make your own means to displace the water in your toilet. Just get one of those 2 liter plastic Coke bottles you can't figure out what to do with, fill it with sand or water, screw on the lid, and put it in your tank.

Where to Get it:
If you want to get a toilet dam, try this source:

Ecological Water Products
102 Aldrich Street
Providence, RI   02905
401/461-0870

72
Volta Batteries

Get some Volta mercury-free, zinc chloride disposable batteries. Mercury is a heavy metal that imposes disastrous effects on our planet. Disposable batteries are the largest source of heavy metal pollution. Mercury is the most common of several heavy metals commonly used in batteries. Mercury poisons our water sources and kills off or causes mutations of fish and other sealife. If we get mercury-free disposable batteries, or better yet, if we get nickel cadmium rechargeable batteries, we can avoid a great deal of pollution.

Planet Saving Benefit:
Volta disposable batteries are better than the mercury based batteries because they do not hurt the environment as dramatically as the "bad" type of mercury batteries.

Money Saving Benefit:
It just so happens that not only are Volta batteries safer for our planet, but they last longer than the "bad" batteries. Volta batteries are available in AA, C, and D sizes. A pack of 4 AA batteries costs $3.95; a pack of 4 D batteries costs $5.50.

Where to Get it:
Some appliance and electronics stores may sell Voltas. Otherwise, get your Volta batteries from this source:

Seventh Generation
49 Hercules Drive,
Colchester, VT 05446.
800/456-1177

73
Wall Switch

Get an automatic wall switch to help you control the amount of energy you use to keep your home illuminated. This switch replaces any regular wall switch (for both incandescent and fluorescent lights), and can be set to automatically turn off between 10 seconds and 7.5 minutes after you leave a room.

Also, automatic wall switches can be set to turn on in the evening, and include a photocell that prevents lights from turning on during daylight hours. You can even override the automatic part of the switch and operate the switch like a regular switch.

Planet Saving Benefit:
It is easy to forget to turn off a light in your home, an act that leads to wasted energy. An automatic wall switch is just one more good way to save energy used for lighting.

Money Saving Benefit:
An automatic wall switch is not cheap, but it is a one-time investment that will pay for itself over time in the energy and money saved. Cost about $20 per automatic wall switch.

Where to Get it:
Get your automatic wall switch at many lighting stores
(retail and commercial), department stores,
hardware stores, and home improvement stores
(the warehouse variety).

74

Washing Machine

Get an energy efficient washing machine. That old washing machine of yours gobbles up about 90% of the energy used to heat water in the water heater. An inefficient washing machine can result in a lot of wasted energy. On top of that, a lot of carbon dioxide is sent into the air needlessly. Manufacturers are building more efficient washing machines, and you and the planet could benefit if you just replace your old machine.

Planet Saving Benefit:

A late model, gas-fueled washing machine can cut your energy use and the amount of carbon dioxide released into the air. In fact, your old machine could be wasting four to eight times more energy compared to the most energy efficient, late model washing machine.

With a new washing machine you can also dramatically cut down on water used by as much as 50%. Why? Because late model washing machines often come with different water level settings, based on the size of your load. For a small load use the lowest water level setting. That way instead of using 40 or 50 gallons to wash, you use perhaps as little as 20 gallons.

Money Saving Benefit:

With your old washing machine you could be squandering up to $100 on utilities every year just because your machine is energy inefficient. So, get an energy efficient one like the Gibson WS 27 M6-V, and bring that expense down to $22 per year. Sears Roebuck also puts out a very energy efficient washing machine: the Sears Roebuck & Co. 4988. Look into it, buy one, and save money over time.

You also save on water cost with one these washing machine, perhaps as much as 40 to 50%.

Where to Get it:

Get your energy efficient washing machine from most major appliance stores and department stores. Ask your appliance merchant about the Gibson appliances. Of course, everyone knows Sears Roebuck. Other well known brands worth checking out include Westinghouse, Frigidaire (yes, they make washing machines), and Maytag.

75
Water Bed Thermostat

Get a water bed thermostat. There are a lot of water beds in this country: 20% of the homes have them. Most of these beds are heated with coils underneath the bed. In fact, heating water beds makes them the most energy consuming thing in the house, even more than the refrigerator and the water heater. This, of course, can make them a threat to the planet by the energy wasted. To control wasted energy, most late model water beds come equipped with a thermostat. But this is not always efficient because the actual temperature level can vary.

To avoid varying temperatures, and reduce wasted energy and expense, install a solid state thermostat that never varies in temperature. This way you can be confident that your water bed will be heated to the exact temperature you wish, no more, no less.

Another good way to conserve energy when you have a water bed is to turn your house heating system down or off on cold nights, and turn up your water bed at night. You will see a significant savings in your energy bill.

Planet Saving Benefit:
These two simple suggestions for your water bed heating can make a big difference in the amount of energy saved. If you happen to have a water bed, there really is no excuse not to do them.

Money Saving Benefit:
A water bed solid state thermostat costs about $100. For about the same price, you may even consider getting an equally efficient device called an energy saver heater, with a built-in reflector. In either case, this type of investment will probably pay for itself in about 1 1/2 years.

Where to Get it:
Get a solid state thermostat or energy saver heater
from the place where you got your water bed.
Or you can try the department stores.

76
Water Heater Insulating Blanket

Get an insulating blanket or jacket for your water heater. Most people have the typical storage tank water heater which has to reheat the water constantly to maintain its temperature. This makes these conventional water heaters energy wasters - up to 30% of your energy bill. You can do one of two things:

* Get a more energy efficient water heater, or

* Get an insulating blanket to insulate your water heater so it does not have to work as hard at maintaining its temperature.

Insulating blankets are an inexpensive alternative to replacing your water heater.

Planet Saving Benefit:
If you insulate your water heater, you make it less of an energy waster. In fact, insulating your water heater, together with turning down your water heater to 120°, can reduce the amount of energy used to about 18% of what it normally takes for it to maintain its temperature. Less energy used spells less expense.

Money Saving Benefit:
An insulating jacket is not a major investment although it can make a major cut in your energy bill. How much for an insulating jacket? About $5 to $20. Your utility company may sell you one for less or perhaps give you one for free.

Where to Get it:
Get an insulating blanket or jacket at most hardware stores and possibly your friendly neighborhood supermarket.

Also, don't forget to call your utility company.

77
Weatherstrip

Get weatherstrip to make your windows more energy efficient. If your windows are old and the wood is chipped and in bad repair, it may be appropriate to invest in insulated windows. However, if your windows are in fairly good shape, you can improve the energy efficiency of your windows by applying weatherstrip.

Weatherstrip comes in several forms, and the type of weatherstrip you use depends on the extent to which you wish to insulate your windows. If you only wish to apply weatherstrip to all the window edges and cracks, just use rope caulk. Otherwise, use either compression or V-strip weatherstrip to caulk the windows.

Planet Saving Benefit:
Weatherstrip applied to windows is a great way to save on energy that would otherwise go out the window - up to 30% of your home's energy. And since there are more windows than doors in most homes, this can lead to substantial energy savings.

Money Saving Benefit:
Rope caulking costs about $1 per window. Compression or V-strip weatherstrip will cost about $8 to $10 per window. This is far cheaper than the $200 to $400 dollars you can spend for each new insulated window. And weatherstrip can actually be just as effective, depending on the window. Which means you could save up to 20% on your energy bill after applying weatherstrip. Weatherstrip: an excellent investment.

Where to Get it:
Get all types of weatherstrip from hardware stores, lumberyards, and home improvement stores.

Personal

As in the list for household and garden things, we provide a list here of alternative products for personal use to take the place of toxic, overpackaged, and non-biodegradable products. We have attempted to identify only the products that we believe are not only safe to our planet and safe for people, but are also of exceptional quality. In other words, the products are very effective, long-lasting, and well made. And, of course, we believe that you will even save some money.

Also, since we are quite concerned about the rights of animals, we have sought to recommend only companies and products that we believe manufacture their wares without testing them on animals.

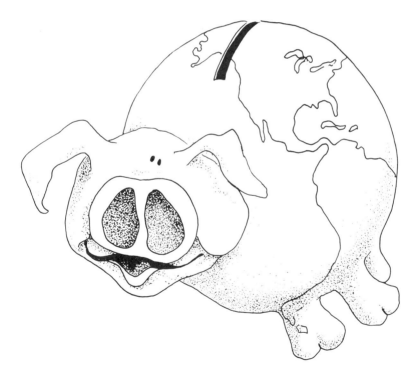

78
Clothes with Natural Fibers

Get clothes with natural fibers rather than clothes made of synthetic fibers. Synthetic fiber clothing means the fiber is made from some type of plastic, usually such things as acrylic, nylon, polyester, or vinyl chloride. Of course, the problem with plastic fibers for clothing is the problem we have with all plastic products: plastic is not biodegradable. Besides that, all plastic comes from non-replenishable petroleum.

The best thing to get for yourself and our planet is clothing made from natural fibers like cotton, silk, or wool. In fact, the best fibers are closely woven, which makes them last longer, and enhances the ability of the fabric to insulate more effectively. Some people are even of the opinion that natural fibers feel nicer.

Planet Saving Benefit:
Clothing made from natural fibers reduces our dependency on synthetic materials, and keeps a certain amount of non-biodegradable products out of our landfills. Also, in most cases, clothing made from natural fibers don't *need* to be dry cleaned. Just learn how to wash your clothes properly. And if you want, you can have a pro press your clean natural fiber garments. By avoiding dry cleaning, you keep a number of very dangerous toxins like perchloroethylene and naphthalene out of the environment.

Money Saving Benefit:
You may or may not save money buying natural fiber clothes. In fact, you may pay a little more than clothes made of man-made fibers. But you may find that well-made clothing made of natural fibers can last a long time. Which makes natural fiber clothing a good investment. Also, as mentioned above, you really can avoid costly dry cleaning by learning to wash natural fiber clothing. Which means you save money.

Where to Get it:
Clothes made of natural fibers are at nearly any clothing store, department store, etc. You can also try this mail order source:

The Cotton Place
P.O. Box 59721
Dallas, TX   75229
800/451-8866

79
Cosmetics

Get natural cosmetics. Cosmetics are usually the products of petroleum. That's right, from oil, black crude. This is a problem because cosmetics draw from a non-replenishable natural energy source. But that's not all. Cosmetics also contain synthetic fragrances and talc. Both of these ingredients are toxic, and talc poses a special problem since it is often tainted with cancer-causing asbestos. And fact is, whatever you apply to your body is absorbed through your skin. Best beware about what you use.

Fortunately, there is a wide variety of natural, non-toxic cosmetics. For example, Paul Penders products include such things as lipsticks, blushers, skin moisturizers, eyeliners, and even make-up removers.

Planet Saving Benefit:
Using natural cosmetics can reduce petroleum use to some extent, and will reduce the amount of toxins thrown into landfills or dumped down the drain.

Money Saving Benefit:
Natural cosmetics and toxic, commercial cosmetics rival each other in cost. Often you can probably get a better deal buying the natural cosmetics. To give you an idea on cost, Paul Pender lipsticks, with many colors to choose from, run about $7.95 for .25 oz; Paul Pender blushers, also in many colors, are about $9.95 for .25 oz.

Where to Get it:
Get natural cosmetics, such as the Paul Pender products, at natural food and ecology stores, or try this source:

Basically Natural
109 East G St.
Brunswick, MD 21716
301/834-7923

80
Cotton Diapers

Get 100% cotton diapers and use a diaper service instead of those plastic disposables. Disposable diapers are not only expensive to buy, but they are costly to our planet. Disposable diapers pose 3 main problems:

- Disposable diapers absorb tens of thousands of tons of raw materials, mostly wood pulp and petroleum-based plastic.

- Disposable diapers take several hundred years to decompose and therefore take up much needed landfill space.

- Disposable diapers threaten our planet with disease because about 50% of these diapers are laden with virus infested excretory matter.

Although disposable diapers are costly, people are enticed by the convenience. We suggest everyone experiment with 100% cotton diapers and a home pickup/dropoff diaper service for a while. Why 100% cotton? Cotton is more healthful for your child, and later on, the diaper service will recycle the diapers.

Planet Saving Benefit:

Cloth diapers are reusable for a long time, and they are biodegradable. When we don't use disposable diapers, we are not wasting trees or our rapidly depleting fossil fuel energy source to produce them. Furthermore, we can reduce whatever risk there may be from the next incurable virus.

By the way, if you opt to buy your own diapers, soak soiled diapers in a mixture of one cup of planet-safe borax and a couple of gallons of warm water. This will get rid of the odor and the stains, and make the diapers more absorbent. For washing, wash diapers in the hottest water possible.

Dry diapers in the sun for further disinfecting.

Money Saving Benefit:

Some people argue this point, but it is very likely that you can save 50% or more on your diaper costs by using cloth diapers and a diaper service. This is a healthy, cheap, and convenient alternative. Why not take advantage of it? To get your own clothe diapers can cost about $30 to $65 for a set of 6. Which you can use over and over again perhaps hundreds of times. Disposable diapers will run you upwards of $600 or more to keep one child in disposable diapers for one year.

Where to Get it:

Fortunately, cloth diapers and diaper services are a growing industry in this country. Check your telephone book for the diaper service in your city. To get your own cloth diapers, try this source:

The Natural Baby Company
RD 1, Box 160
Titusville, NJ   08560
800/388-BABY

81
Deodorant

Get a natural alternative to replace your toxic, commercial deodorant. Deodorants contain several toxic ingredients. One ingredient is formaldehyde, which is a known carcinogen. Another ingredient is the aluminum salts that are toxic and that some medical experts believe may contribute to such brain problems as Alzheimer's disease. Then there is the other problem of the aerosol spray deodorants, which just send out CFCs or other aerosol propellants to ruin the depleting ozone layer.

You do not need to expose yourself to the chemicals in deodorants, nor is it necessary to expose our planet or our planet's atmosphere to anything ruinous. Why? Because there are several very effective, non-toxic, natural alternatives to address the problem of trying to smell nice.

Try baking soda. Yes, this remarkable mineral can literally absorb wetness and deodorize your body. Just pinch some straight from the box and apply where needed. Another interesting alternative is a 100% natural deodorant crystal. It just looks like a large, transparent rock that you moisten and then apply to your skin. It works! There are also effective roll-ons available made from such wholesome things as the camomile herb and the aloe vera plant.

Planet Saving Benefit:
We can keep a certain percentage of toxins away from us and our planet just by using natural alternatives to the toxic deodorants. The natural alternatives also prevent various aerosol propellants from escaping into the atmosphere.

Money Saving Benefit:
The toxic, commercial deodorants are not cheap. But baking soda is cheap, and such things as crystals are, too, when you consider that a crystal weighs less than 4 ounces and for only $7 can last 1 to 2 years.

Where to Get it:

Get baking soda at the supermarket. Get deodorant crystals at your health food store, ecology shop, or try this source:

EveryBody Ltd.
1738 Pearl St.
Boulder, CO 80302
303/440-0188

82
Soap

Get a natural soap into your home. You may be surprised to know that most commercial soaps are toxic. Among other things, soaps often contain such things as ammonia, formaldehyde, and phenol (these last two ingredients are considered to be cancer-causing). Often added to this are synthetic fragrances that can stink so much, that's all you smell. Some people even react to these fragrances, breaking out into a rash.

Just dispense with the toxic stuff, and get natural soaps that are better for you and our planet. Non-toxic soaps are made from a variety of natural ingredients. They may be anything from olive and coconut oil extracts to honey, flowers, and herbs. In all cases they are usually very effective soaps and pleasant to smell.

Planet Saving Benefit:
By not using toxic commercial soaps, we don't send toxic and possibly cancer-causing chemicals down the drain. This keeps toxins out of our water tables and other places on our planet.

Money Saving Benefit:
Very often natural soaps last longer than the commercial, toxic variety. Why? Probably because the commercial product is designed to be used up faster so you'll go out and buy more of their product. Aren't they clever... You may pay up to twice the cost for natural soaps as you would for regular commercial soap, but the investment is worth it. Rokeach Coconut Oil Soap is $1.09 for a 3.0 oz. bar; Pure Almond Oil Castile Soap is $1.00 for a 4.0 oz. bar.

Where to Get it:
Get natural soap at nearly any natural food or ecology store. Or, you can try this source to get each of the soaps mentioned above:

The Ecology Box
425 East Washington, #202
Ann Arbor, MI   48104
800/735-1371

83
Un-Petroleum Jelly

Get un-petroleum jelly as an alternative to your petroleum jelly. Petroleum jelly is exactly what the name implies: it is derived from petroleum. Here again is another product that exploits a non-replenishable resource.

The alternative to petroleum jelly is something called un-petroleum jelly. Interestingly enough, although this product is not petroleum-based, it works just as effectively as the petroleum-based product. The difference is that un-petroleum jelly uses all natural ingredients like castor, soy, and almond oils, combined with beeswax, palm wax, and sumac berry wax. Vitamin E is even added to help heal diaper rash if applied to your baby's rump.

Planet Saving Benefit:
Using replenishable alternatives to petroleum products is another good way to control our use of petroleum. Besides, with un-petroleum jelly, nothing but good stuff is reabsorbed back into our planet.

Money Saving Benefit:
Since you get 2 products in one - one to lubricate, and the other to heal - you are making a good investment with un-petroleum jelly. The cost: less than $6 for one 4 oz. jar. An investment which could last a long time.

Where to Get it:
Get un-petroleum jelly at many natural food shops and ecology stores. Or you can try this mail order source:

Basically Natural
109 East G St.
Brunswick, MD   21716
301/834-7923

Automotive

Nearly everyone is aware of such things as smog, much of which is attributed to cars. But smog is only part of the problem with cars, albeit a very serious problem. There is, of course, the incredible, unreplenishable amount of fossil fuels burned up by cars (some 200 million gallons per day of gas in America alone). But what about the other resources exploited for cars?

Think about it: there are about 140 million cars in America, and each car weighs about half a ton. This means a half ton of raw materials, which includes steel, glass, rubber, and plastic, goes into each of the 140 million cars. That's a tremendous amount of resources. And since most cars are just thrown away, these are resources that will never go back into our planet. Consider just tires alone - at this time about a quarter of a billion tires are just sitting on various landfills all over the country.

Added to these horrible things is the fact that cars use batteries, which are a source of tons of sulfuric acid and lead leaking onto our planet from disposed cars. This does not even include the millions of gallons of oil, transmission fluid, coolant, etc., which also leak from cars (disposed and non-disposed alike).

Listed here are a few ways you can help save our planet by making your car more fuel efficient, and by keeping batteries, tires, and even your car out of landfills a lot longer.

84
Air Pressure Gauge

Get an air pressure gauge for your car. You may not think there is much of a connection between your car's tire air pressure and fuel efficiency. But the fact is that when you drive your car with tires that are not inflated enough, this actually creates resistance, and puts added strain on your engine. The result is that it takes more gas to keep you mobile. The way to deal with this is to find out the optimum tire pressure for your car's tires, and get a tire pressure gauge to check your tires every other week or so. Then just inflate your tires as needed.

How do you use a tire pressure gauge? It's easy. Just remove the rubber thimble that covers the air valve on each tire, then take the tire gauge and press the round end with the little pin in the center over the air valve. The air in the tire will immediately cause a little measuring stick to shoot out of the other end of the gauge. Check for the pounds per square inch (PSI). The proper PSI varies for different cars. Just consult your car manual, or call your car dealer.

Planet Saving Benefit:
Properly inflated tires mean less fossil fuel is wasted to keep your car mobile. And more fossil fuel now means more fossil fuel later. In fact, if everyone kept his tires inflated properly, as much as 2 billion gallons of fuel per year could be saved.

Another benefit is that you won't wear out your tires as fast, which means you don't have to replace them as often.

Money Saving Benefit:
You can pick up an air pressure gauge for under $2. This will help you check your air pressure regularly, and save you money because your car will operate more fuel efficiently. You may save up to 5% or more on gas expenses. Every little bit helps. And since your tires last longer, you save on this expense, too.

Where to Get it:
Get your pressure gauge from your friendly neighborhood gas station, discount store, or department store in the auto department. You may even try getting a free pressure gauge from your car dealer.

85
Car Batteries

Get into the habit of going to service stations that recycle old car batteries. Car batteries are a horrendous source of pollution to our planet. Car batteries consist almost entirely of lead and sulfuric acid. In fact, car batteries use nearly 71% of the lead used in this country. Over 65 million car batteries end up in landfills each year. And of course, their highly toxic substances seep into our water supplies.

You may not be able to live entirely without the manufacturing of new car batteries as long as society continues to use cars. But we can at least make an attempt to recycle these awful things by taking them to a service station that recycles dead car batteries.

Planet Saving Benefit:
Recycling car batteries is one way to keep them out of landfills. Ultimately, such a practice can help keep out terrible toxins that are making our water supplies undrinkable.

Money Saving Benefit:
If you can find a service station that recycles car batteries, chances are that you will get credit toward the purchase of your next battery at that station. A few pennies saved are a few pennies earned.

Where to Get it:
Unfortunately, the decline in the price of lead has resulted in fewer places that recycle car batteries. 25 years ago, 97% of batteries were recycled, now it's at 80% at best.

Call around to find a service station that does recycle car batteries; sooner or later you'll find one.

86
Fuel Efficient Car

Get a fuel efficient car. There are a number of well made, safe, fuel efficient cars on the market these days. There does seem to be a trend for automakers to introduce more large cars now than they have since the "energy conscious" '70s. On the whole, however, cars now are being engineered to save on gas.

One way to ensure fuel economy is to get a new car with a standard transmission versus an automatic. Standard transmissions are still more fuel efficient than automatic transmissions.

There are some solar-electric powered cars on the market. For example, Solar Car Corporation in Melbourne, Florida, came out with a car in the early part of 1991 with a list price of $25,000. The car is designed to operate just like a regular car (same acceleration, handling, etc.), only using the sun's power and a battery bank in place of gas. Unfortunately, this car may still be somewhat out of range for most people's budgets.

Planet Saving Benefit:
The more fuel efficient your car, the less fossil fuel is wasted and the less exhaust is spewed into the air.

Money Saving Benefit:
Usually, fuel efficient cars cost less when you buy them, and can operate more economically because it costs less each time you tank up for gas.

Where to Get it:
To choose the most fuel efficient car (based on model type and car engine size), we recommend you send away for the latest copy of the U.S. Department of Energy's *Gas Mileage Guide*. Send for your *free* copy at:

Consumer Information Center
Pueblo, CO 81009

87
Rebuilt Engine

Get the engine of your car rebuilt rather than buying a new car. Cars are not getting any cheaper to buy, and they are not getting any less costly from the standpoint of the energy and resources needed to manufacture new cars. For the 9 million or more cars taken to the junk pile each year, we waste the equivalent of 10 billion tons of resources (including steel, glass, etc., and the incredible amount of energy expended) which went into making them. That means 1,000 tons of resources per car! That's a lot of resources squandered for a disposable item.

Obviously, if we hang on to our cars longer, the need for new cars and the number of cars junked are reduced.

There really is no need to throw away an entire car that only needs some new parts and an engine. The problem is that in a throw-away society, getting rid of the old clunker for something new and better looking has been too enticing. This is just one more of those bad habits Americans should learn to shake loose.

Planet Saving Benefit:
A rebuilt engine means a longer life for your car. This also means one less object weighing a half ton or better is thrown away somewhere, robbing diminishing landfill space, and robbing our planet of diminishing resources.

Money Saving Benefit:
Rebuilding your engine may cost only a few hundred dollars. Which is a distinct cost difference compared to several thousand dollars to buy a new or even a late model used car. Also, your rebuilt engine can keep your car running another 50,000 or more miles.

Where to Get it:
Get your engine rebuilt by a local engine rebuilder.

Look for one in the telephone book under
Engines - Rebuilding, Repairing, & Exchanging.

88
Recycled Oil Change

Get a regular oil change, preferably using recycled oil. Recycled oil? Yes. Over the years, the oil companies have led you all to believe that oil used for lubricating our cars is a use once, throw away proposition. The outcome of this thinking is that each year Americans dispose of 350 million gallons of oil. This is hazardous and wasteful. After all, oil is highly toxic, and is not replenishable once dumped. However, there is a process that can not only recycle used motor oil, but also can produce oil that is as good as if not better than the original virgin oil.

Planet Saving Benefit:

If you all start using recycled oil, and enough of you insist on it wherever you go, those millions of gallons of improperly disposed oil can be kept out of the environment. Not only that, but if you get a regular oil change, your car will operate more efficiently, and fewer greenhouse gases will be dumped into the atmosphere. Moreover, your car will last longer, which saves energy, resources, and landfill space.

In Houston, EXXON has recently begun a program to accept used oil from planet-conscious consumers. This is a good planet-saving move. So far the program has met with overwhelming success.

Money Saving Benefit:

Like a regular tune-up for your car, a regular oil change will make your car run more efficiently, which cuts down on fuel costs, and increases the lifespan of your car. While you're at it, you may as well get the oil changed with recycled oil.

Where to Get it:

Where do you get this stuff? At quick oil change shops (although not all use recycled oil yet). These days nearly every city has one. Check around to find one that uses recycled oil. The quick oil change shops also provide the used oil to the oil recycler. One noted oil recycler in this country on the WestCoast is Evergreen Oil, Inc. On the East Coast is another company: CAM2 Oil Products Company. To get CAM2 motor oil by mail order, contact them at:

CAM2 Oil Products Company
380 West Butler Ave., New Britain, PA 18901
800/338-2262

89
Retreaded Tires

Get retreaded tires. Tires are a bigger hazard to our planet than most people realize. To begin with, tires require a lot of energy and crude oil to manufacture (about 1/2 barrel of crude for one tire). Later on, after the tires have done their duty, they are often just thrown into landfills. The problem is that tires are not biodegradable, so they just sit there.

To avoid the growing mountain of tires (which runs into the billions of tires at this point), you should buy only retreaded tires. Of course, you can get radial or steel belted tires which tend to last longer, and can increase your car's gas efficiency by 10%. Make sure, however, that you purchase retreaded tires from a reputable, well-known source. Poorly manufactured retreaded tires can be hazardous. Also, find out the maximum speed for which the tires are rated. Moderate speeds and gentle handling can prevent undue wear and tear on retreads.

Planet Saving Benefit:
Retreading tires extend the life of tires, and can reduce the number of tires dumped into landfills.

Money Saving Benefit:
Usually retreaded tires are cheaper than new tires. Also, the longer you keep your tires, the fewer tires you may have to buy in your lifetime. And if you get radial or steel belted tires, you save on fuel cost.

Where to Get it:
Retreaded tires are available at most decent tire stores, auto parts shops, or auto service centers. Sometimes you may have to ask specifically about retreaded tires.

Remember: the tire salesman makes more money
if he can sell you a new tire.

90
Tune-up

Get a regular tune-up for your car. Cars are great fossil fuel wasters. Added to that, cars produce a great deal of carbon dioxide gas that is responsible for global warming and all the climatic problems that global warming yields. As hard as it might seem to believe, if you all tuned up your cars regularly (about once every 12,000 to 15,000 miles), you could dramatically reduce the amount of fuel wasted and carbon dioxide released into the environment.

Planet Saving Benefit:
Tune-ups make our cars run more efficiently. This results in less fuel consumption, and reduces the amount of carbon dioxide dumped into the air every day. Right now Americans consume more than 200 million gallons of gas per day. You can cut down this fuel consumption by 10% with regular tune-ups. Regular tune-ups can also prevent about 400,000,000 pounds of carbon dioxide from being released into the atmosphere every day.

Money Saving Benefit:
Tune up your car regularly, and you won't have to retank your car as often. This means you won't be paying out as much in gas. But what about the expense for the tune-up? These days there are specialty tune-up services which give regular tune-up specials. Take advantage of them. You may find that what you spend for a tune-up is more than repaid in gas you don't have to buy.

Also, a regular tune-up (and oil change for that matter) will extend the life of your car.

Where to Get it:
Get a tune-up at any of those quick oil, lube, and tune-up service operations. They're cheap and quick. And many of them recycle the oil they collect from customers.

91
VitalizeR

Get a VitalizeR for your car, truck, boat, or motorcycle. A VitalizeR is a cylinder-shaped device that you connect to the fuel line of your vehicle. The manufacturer and many enthusiastic users of the VitalizeR support the following statistics. The Vitalizer will:

- increase gas mileage up to 23%
- decrease exhaust emissions up to 90%
- decrease carbon monoxide emissions by 57%
- increase engine life
- decrease the frequency of the need for oil changes/tune-ups
- increase acceleration power.

The key to using the VitalizeR successfully is to install it correctly. If the VitalizeR is not installed correctly, it may not work effectively. Once properly installed, the VitalizeR causes electrostatically charged fuel molecules to disburse efficiently, which makes the fuel burn more efficiently. The end result is greater force against the pistons, which yields greater power and fuel economy.

Planet Saving Benefit:
This clever device can dramatically reduce the amount of fuel needed to keep your car running, and greatly reduce the amount of carbon monoxide dumped into the atmosphere. Also, since fewer oil changes are needed, less oil is used and ultimately poured into our water sources.

Money Saving Benefit:
Compared to the potential cash you can save in what you won't have to spend for gas, oil, and tune-ups, the VitalizeR is a bargain at only $129. You can install the VitalizeR yourself (it takes about 15 to 60 minutes), or have your mechanic install it for you. The VitalizeR can be used for cars that run on leaded, unleaded, or diesel fuels.

Where to Get it:
Get your VitalizeR at this source:

Karen's Nontoxic Products
1839 Dr. Jack Road, Conowingo, MD   21918
301/378-4621

Other

The list presented here includes a few things you should know about. The emphasis is on recycling, and here are some suggestions on things you can recycle or adopt as part of your recycling efforts. Also, the aim here is to inspire creative ways to use recycled and reusable products to avoid having to use products that waste diminishing resources.

Don't forget that people need to concern themselves with plants and trees. Plants and trees are very important to the survival of our planet, to people, and to animals. There *is* something we can do about the rainforests and the trees we rely on for paper needs.

92
Can Crusher

Get a can crusher to crush your aluminum cans. You should get into the planet-saving habit of recycling. Although Americans are recycling about 60% of the aluminum cans produced every year, you can do better. To help you in your effort to recycle aluminum cans, get a can crusher.

The can crusher looks like an old fashioned nut cracker. Only instead of cracking nuts, you crush cans. The fact is that the can crusher makes crushing cans much easier, and the crushed cans make it possible for you to store more cans in your recycling storage bin. This helps save on the number of trips you make to the recycling center, which means you burn less gas getting there.

Planet Saving Benefit:
It is more healthful for our planet to recycle aluminum than to have to manufacture new aluminum for new cans. One ton of aluminum requires nearly 9,000 pounds of bauxite and 1,020 pounds of petroleum coke. Recycling aluminum cans reduces the need for raw material by 95%, and reduces the energy needed to produce aluminum by 90%. The can crusher will make the habit of recycling aluminum much more convenient, and this is helpful.

Money Saving Benefit:
You may not make big bucks saving, crushing, and recycling aluminum cans, but it's always a nice feeling when you drop off a bunch of cans and walk away with money in your pocket. Besides, a can crusher is not a big expense at $9.

Where to Get it:
Get your can crusher at some home improvement stores
(the warehouse variety), ecology shops,
discount stores, and hardware stores.

93
Greeting Cards

Get greeting cards made from recycled paper, or make your own out of recycled paper. When we use recycled paper products over products made from virgin paper, we save trees, we avoid using energy and water needed to manufacture virgin paper, and we don't add to the highly toxic dioxins dumped into rivers near paper mills.

You may not think you're much of an artist, but it really is the thought that counts when we give greeting cards to people. Try just keeping your messages simple. For example, for a birthday just say: "HAPPY Birthday! You're 30 today. You're not as far over the hill as you may think."

When making your own greeting cards, consider using non-toxic, water-soluble inks, markers, and paints.

It is easy to identify greeting cards made from recycled paper. Just look for the recycled symbol. Be aware, however, that the *recycled* symbol is distinctly different from the *recyclable* symbol. Recycled means the product is actually made from recycled products; Recyclable means the product can be recycled into a recycled product.

Planet Saving Benefit:
Recycled greeting cards don't take up landfill space and waste non-renewable resources. The only draw-back is that the recycled paper may be bleached to create whiteness.

Money Saving Benefit:
If you use recycled paper to make your own greeting cards, you'll be delighted to know that the paper is cheaper than the paper made from virgin sources. Cost: $3 or less per ream (500 sheets).

Where to Get it:
Hallmark Cards are often made from recycled/recyclable paper. These cards are usually available at nearly any stationery store that carries greeting cards. They can also be found at pharmacies, discount stores, and many supermarkets.

94
Live Christmas Tree

Get a live potted Christmas tree. If you happen to celebrate Christmas every year, like so many Americans, chances are you buy a cut one. The problem with this is that millions of trees are wasted, trees that are only appreciated for a few short weeks (if that long), only to be thrown away. Not only that, but many of these trees are sprayed with toxic preservatives and "snow" that only seeps into our water sources.

This year, try celebrating with a live potted tree. A live tree can be enjoyed every year for years to come, and it works year-round to gobble up greenhouse gases. It also smells good indoors, and does not dump its needles like a drying cut tree does. Eventually, you can plant your live Christmas tree, and get another one to carry on the tradition and contribute to a healthier planet.

Planet Saving Benefit:
Any plant or tree you get and care for is a beneficial contribution to our planet. You don't waste cut trees, and you discourage the use of the toxic junk cut Christmas tree peddlers put on these trees.

In Louisiana, citizens recycle cut Christmas trees after the holiday season to help retard coastal wetlands erosion. Thousands of trees are placed in pen-like enclosures in shallow coastal waters to slow down currents and trap sediments. This process eventually builds new wetlands.

Money Saving Benefit:
Live Christmas trees are a sound investment. For one thing, they do not cost much more than a cut tree, and you save money over the years by not buying cut trees year after year.

Where to Get it:
If you look around, many nurseries sell Christmas trees such as Douglas fir or spruce year-round. In some cases, they get a special shipment in just for the season.

Check your telephone book
and call up a few nurseries in your city.

95
Old Paint Brushes

Get out your old paint brushes if you still have them, and renew them. Most people paint sooner or later. And most people end up with paint brushes encrusted with paint. Unfortunately, these old crusty paint brushes end up in a landfill somewhere. This is not necessary if you just renew your old paint brushes using the following simple procedure:

- Get a saucepan you don't plan to use again for cooking, and get out your old brushes.

- Put the brushes into the pan and submerge them in white vinegar.

- Bring this concoction to a boil, turn down heat, and allow to simmer for several minutes.

- Remove brushes from the pan and wash them in soap and water until the brushes are clean.

Don't throw the saucepan away. There will probably be other occasions when you can use it for brushes or for some other household chore.

Planet Saving Benefit:
When renewing old brushes, you can use them over and over for a long time. This means you are not throwing brush upon brush into landfills. This saves space in the landfills, and also spares the planet from the toxic paint products that would invariably come from paint brushes sitting in a landfill. Moreover, fewer brushes have to be made from non-renewable resources.

Money Saving Benefit:
Using inexpensive white vinegar and inexpensive hot water (especially if heated on a gas stove) is cheaper than throwing away and replacing paint brushes.

Where to Get it:
White vinegar is at your supermarket, and everyone has an old sauce pan he's thinking of throwing out. If not, buy a cheap one at a yard sale or a pawn shop.

96
Paint

Get a non-hazardous, low-odor, water base paint the next time you want to paint your home. Paint has been a great hazard to our planet. Most of its ingredients are toxic, and many are cancer-causing, including such things as benzene, formaldehyde, lead, pentachlorophenol, phenol, toluene, xylene, etc. This stuff ends up in landfills, and eventually ends up in our water sources. If we can use alternatives, we should use them.

Fortunately, AFM Enterprises, Inc., manufactures alternatives to the toxic, commercial paints. The product is called *Safecoat*. You can start by using the *Safecoat Primer Undercoater* to be applied to wood or most wall surfaces. Then you choose a Safecoat paint that is either flat, semi-gloss, or gloss according to your preference. These products come in white and bone, but you can add color by tinting to any light to medium shade using any universal water base tinting system.

Planet Saving Benefit:
Since *Safecoat* paints are designed for the purpose of keeping hazardous chemicals from polluting our planet, this is a product worth using. Use of this product will prevent further exploitation of our water sources, and harm to people, plants, and animals.

Money Saving Benefit:
Safecoat paints are not only safe to use, but for the quality of the paint, some may consider them cheaper than the hazardous variety. And since you can use any universal water base tinting system, you can create any color you want. The variations are endless. Cost? A gallon of flat *Safecoat* paint: $25.25.

Where to Get it:
Get *Safecoat* paint from this source:

AFM Enterprises
1140 Stacy Court
Riverside, CA 92507
714/781-6860

97

Plants

Get plants. Plants are not only beautiful to look at, they can be very beneficial to our lives and certainly to our planet. It is believed by some researchers that, with enough indoor plants, you can actually purify the air. Apparently, the best plants to achieve this are such plants as mother-in-law's tongue and spider plants.

Planet Saving Benefit:

Outdoors, if each of you plants a tree, that tree in time can consume 13 pounds of carbon dioxide per year. Obviously, if all Americans planted one tree each, a significant amount of carbon dioxide could be eliminated. To give you some idea, one million mature trees (13 years or older) could eliminate 100 million pounds of carbon dioxide per year.

Money Saving Benefit:

If you use plants to purify your home, you can save on buying toxic deodorizers or air fresheners. If you plant trees around your house in the right places, you can cut down your cooling bill by up to 50% because of the shade. If you decide to plant fruit trees, you can save money on the produce these trees will yield. And don't forget vegetable gardening, that's another way to save money (and eat healthy!).

In either case, plants are never a bad investment, and can possibly save you a buck or two.

Where to Get it:

Get plants or trees at your nursery; you'll get advice on how easy planting is. Even many supermarkets are selling a variety of plants these days. To get information on growing trees or edible plants from organically grown seeds, try this source:

Northwoods Nursery
28696 South Cramer Rd.
Molalla, OR 97038
503/651-3737

98
Monkey Globe

Get a Monkey Globe. A Monkey what? Something has to be said about the horrendous destruction of the planet's rainforests. They are either cut down for cattle grazing, or burned, or whatnot. This poses a direct threat to the very survival of the planet and its inhabitants.

Why? For a number of reasons. For one thing, the rainforests actually generate a great deal of oxygen that people and animals need to live. For another thing, the rainforests are important for absorbing carbon dioxide which threatens the planet. For yet one more thing, a third of the planet's animals and insect species live in the rainforests and are facing rapid extinction because of what is going on there.

A Monkey Globe is a globe made of fabric which, when turned inside out, turns into a furry, cuddly toy monkey. Getting one of these toys from the Friends of the Forest contributes money used to preserve the rainforests.

Planet Saving Benefit:
Money used to preserve the planet means you get to live here a little longer.

Money Saving Benefit:
Sooner or later everyone needs to get a gift for someone. Consider it an investment in our hurting planet. For a measly $21.95, you can get a Monkey Globe. Surely the planet and someone you love is worth that much.

Where to Get it:
Get your Monkey Globe from:

Friends of the Forest
41 Madison Ave., 36th Floor
New York, NY   10010
212/689-7500

You may also want to contact and support the efforts of this organization:

Rainforest Action Network
301 Broadway,
Suite A
San Francisco, CA   94133
415/398-4404

99
Products in Glass Jars

Get products in glass jars whenever possible, especially as an alternative to plastic. Glass is a recyclable resource that we should take advantage of. Plastic is not biodegradable, and does not recycle very easily.

You can drop any color of glass at your recycling center, but deliver preferably only bottles and jars, without any metal on them. Dishes, glass from windows, and light bulbs don't count because they contain non-recyclable additives.

Also, if you buy glass jars, they are a means to store things. Jars can be good for storing food leftovers, even dry foods like pasta, rice, and beans. Or you can use them to store nails, thumb tacks, paper clips, and many other things. The point is that there is no need to go out and buy containers. This system keeps glass jars and bottles out of the landfills.

Planet Saving Benefit:

When we recycle the glass jars that we use, we are recycling a product that can be recycled infinitely. Recycling saves landfill space. Otherwise, it takes several thousand years for a bottle to decompose. Recycling glass saves on using raw resources, and the energy needed to make new glass. And by the way, returnable bottle programs are very effective: 90% of the bottles get returned.

Money Saving Benefit:

When you get products in glass jars or bottles, chances are you can use the jars or bottles as reusable storage containers for various things. This way you save by not having to buy storage containers. And if you live in a state where they have a returnable bottle program, by all means, get the money for your returnable bottles.

Where to Get it:

Glass jars and bottles are used to contain many different types of products. Most of these products are found on your supermarket shelves.

100
Unfinished Solid Wood Furniture

Get unfinished, solid wood furniture. Solid wood furniture is good to get because it is non-toxic and biodegradable. It is also a very efficient use of trees because you can have wood furniture for your lifetime, and even pass the furniture on to your heirs.

However, when getting wood furniture, most people do not realize that what is claimed to be solid wood furniture is often limited to pieces of solid wood hiding mostly particle board and veneered plywood. The problem is that particle board and plywood contain toxic, cancer-causing formaldehyde that easily escapes (out-gasses) into the environment. This type of furniture also is flimsy and gets discarded after a few years - into landfills.

When buying wood furniture, try to get unfinished solid wood furniture. This makes it easier to spot particle board or plywood components. Plus, you can stain the wood with natural, non-toxic, or low-toxic stains.

Planet Saving Benefit:
Solid wood furniture (without formaldehyde) will not hurt our planet. And if you pass it on, it won't take up landfill space.

Money Saving Benefit:
The nice thing about furniture is that you can get it used. This means you buy something that did not waste more raw material, but it also means it's usually cheaper. The obvious exception would be antiques, though their value increases over time, making them a good investment. New, unfinished solid wood furniture can save you money, because some of the labor to manufacture the furniture has been eliminated. Well-made solid wood furniture is a good investment because you may never have to replace it.

Where to Get it:
Get unfinished or used wood furniture from many specialty furniture stores. Check your telephone book for Furniture Dealers.

101
Recycling Boxes or Bins

Get recycling boxes or containers in which to temporarily store items intended for recycling. Naturally, a book like this cannot avoid mentioning the necessity for everyone to contribute to recycling. There is much, after all, that can and should be recycled. The problem for most people about recycling are:

• Knowing how to get their recyclable items into the recycling system

• Managing their recyclable items.

To find out how to get your recyclable items into the recycling system, simply contact your local garbage collection department. Ask them for information about a recycling center that may be in your area. You may be surprised, some cities offer curbside pickup. Others will direct you to a recycling center.

Managing your recyclable items is just a matter of organizing your recyclable items into five broad groups (sometimes more):

• Paper (especially newspapers, garbage bags, cardboard, etc.)
• Plastic (soda bottles, milk bottles, etc.)
• Aluminum
• Other metals (anything made of metal except cans with lead)
• Glass (soda bottles, food jars, etc.)

Bear in mind that Styrofoam does not qualify as plastic. There is nothing you can do with this stuff, as it never decomposes. It is best to just not buy anything made of Styrofoam.

Aluminum is in its own group because there is so much of the stuff around, and it makes it easier for the recycler if you provide aluminum separate from other metals.

As for metal with lead, this usually comes in the form of only certain tin cans. You can identify lead on a tin can by the bluish color of a metal band that extends along the side of the can.

Also, different plastics are recycled differently, and what you collect may or may not be accepted by your recycling center. You may even have to separate plastics. Remember: when in doubt, call ahead to your recycler to confirm what they accept and how they want it delivered.

To help manage your recyclables, get 5 (or more if needed) boxes or plastic trash cans (for outdoor storage). Each box should be designated for a particular group of recyclables (e.g., plastics go in the box designated for plastics, paper goes in the box designated for paper, etc.). Then, when most of all the boxes are full, either call for pickup, wait for the pickup day, or go to the recycling center.

Planet Saving Benefit:
Recycling as much as we can reduces the amount of raw material needed to manufacture new things, which means less energy is used for manufacturing. Everyone should recycle as much as possible.

Money Saving Benefit:
Recycling can not only become a planet-beneficial practice, but it could even be a money-making opportunity. The fact is certain recyclable items are worth money and you can cash in on what you have collected. Aluminum, for example, is one of the most common money-making recyclables.

Where to Get it:
Get boxes at your local supermarket. Or get durable, flexible, plastic trash cans with lids for your storage bins. Otherwise, you can get a recycling bin and information on recycling from this source:

Home Recycling Catalogue
2141 P Street NW
Suite 204
Washington, DC   20037
202/331-9578

Sources

Here is the list of sources used to create this book. They are recommended to those who wish to consult them for more information on things covered in this book.

A Consumer's Dictionary of Cosmetic Ingredients, Ruth Winter (New York, Crown, 1984)

Alternatives to Landfilling Household Toxins, Gina Purin, Judy Orttung, Stephen van Stockum, and Janet Page (Sacramento, Golden Empire Health Planning Center, 1986)

Become an Environmental Shopper, Pennsylvania Resources Council (Media, PA)

Consumer Guide to Home Energy Savings, Alex Wilson (The American Council for an Energy-Efficient Economy, 1990)

Healthful Houses: How to Design and Build Your Own, Clint Good with Debra Lynn Dadd (Bethesda, MD, Guaranty Press, 1988)

HHWP's Guide to Hazardous Products Around the Home, Household Hazardous Waste Project (Southwest Missouri State University, 1989)

The Household Pollutants Guide, Albert J. Fritsch (Garden City, NY, Anchor Books, 1978)

How to Clean Practically Anything, Monte Florman (Mount Vernon, NY, Consumer Reports Books, Consumer Union, 1986)

Keep Your Pet Healthy the Natural Way, Pat Lazarus (New Canaan, CT, Keats Publishing, 1983)

The Natural Garden, Ken Druse (New York, Clarkson N. Potter, 1989)

Nontoxic, Natural, & Earthwise, Debra Lynn Dadd (Los Angeles, Jeremy P. Tarcher, Inc., 1990)

Places Rated Almanac, Richard Boyer & David Savageau (New York, Prentice Hall, 1989)

Oil and Gas Heating Systems, Maintenance and Improvement. (Environmental Science Department of Massachusetts Audubon Society, January 1990)

The Recycler's Handbook, The Earthworks Group (Berkeley, The Earthworks Press, Inc.)

Shopping For a Better World: A Quick and Easy Guide to Socially Responsible Supermarket Shopping, (New York, Ballantine Books, 1990)

50 Simple Things Your Business Can Do to Save The Earth, The Earthworks Group (Berkeley, The Earthworks Press, Inc., 1991)

50 Simple Things You Can Do to Save The Earth, The Earthworks Group (Berkeley, The Earthworks Press, Inc., 1989)

State of the World A World Watch Institute Report on Progress Toward a Sustainable Society, Lester R. Brown (New York, W.W. Norton, 1989)

Water Efficiency for Your Home, Rocky Mountain Institute (Snowmass, CO)

This book recommends the following magazines:

The Environmental Magazine, P.O. Box 6667, Syracuse, NY, 13217
800/825-0061

Home Energy, 2124 Kittredge St., No. 95, Berkeley, CA, 94704

Garbage, P.O. Box 56519, Boulder CO 80322
800/274-9909

This book encourages the reader to contact the following organizations:

American Council for an Energy-Efficient Economy
1001 Connecticut Ave. NW
Suite 535
Washington, DC 20036
202/429-8873

Association for Commuter Transportation
808 17th St., NW
#200
Washington, DC 20006
202/659-0602

Clean Water Action
317 Pennsylvania Ave., SE
Washington, DC 20003
202/547-1196

Conservation & Renewable Energy,
Inquiry & Referral Service
P.O. Box 8900
Silver Springs, MD 20904
800/523-2929

Council on Economic Priorities
30 Irving Place
New York, NY 10003
212/420-1133

Foliage for Clean Air Council
405 N Washington St.
Falls Church, VA 22046
703/241-4004

Friends of the Earth
218 D. St., SE
Washington, DC 20003
202/544-2600

Greenhouse Crisis Foundation
1130 17th St., NW
Suite 630
Washington, DC 20036
202/466-2823

Greenpeace
1636 U St. NW
Washington, DC 20009
202/462-1177

101 Ways To Save Money & Save Our Planet ❦ *137*

Household Hazardous Waste Project
P.O. Box 108
Springfield, MO 65804
417/836-5777

National Coalition Against the Misuse of Pesticides
530 Seventh St., SE
Washington, DC 20003
202/534-5450

The Nature Conservancy
1815 N Lynn St.
Arlington, VA 22209
703/841-2907

Rainforest Action Network
301 Broadway
Suite A
San Francisco, CA 94133
415/398-4404

Sierra Club
Dept. H-113
P.O. Box 7959
San Francisco, CA
94120-7959

Index

A

Acid rain, 49
Adjustable radiator vent, 83
Aerosol propellants, 15, 34, 10
AFM Enterprises, Inc., 28, 53, 126
Air conditioner, 67
Air fresheners, 12, 127
Air pressure gauge, 112
Allergic reactions, 47
Aluminum cans, 122
Alzheimer's disease, 106
Ammonia, 26, 28, 31, 36, 48, 108
Artificial dyes, 24
Automatic wall switch, 95

B

Baking soda, 25, 26, 31, 34, 40, 46, 106
Basically Natural, 103, 109
Basil, 32
Battery recharger, 50
Benzene, 16, 37, 126
Biodegradable, 11, 15, 18, 39, 44, 105, 117, 130, 131
Biodegradable floor cleaners, 28
Biomat Airspray, 15
Black coffee, 42
Blood stains, 16
Booster heater, 60
Borax, 16, 20, 24, 46
Brass, 31
Bronze, 31
Burns, 34, 48
Butane, 15

C

CAM2 Oil Products Company, 116
Can crusher, 122
Cancer-causing toxins, 47
Car batteries, 113
Carbon dioxide, 73, 82, 118, 127
Carbon monoxide, 119

Carpet spot remover, 16
Cars, 114
Carpool, 54
Caulking and spackling, 53
Cedar blocks, 17
Cellulose insulation, 52
Cellulose sponges, 44
Central air conditioning system, 56
Chemicals, 11, 12
Chlorine bleach, 26
Chlorofluorocarbons, 11
Chrome, 31
Citronella candles, 32
Clean Country, 25
Clean Environments, 14
Clothcrafters, 22
Clothesline, 26, 58
Coastal wetlands erosion, 124
Commuting, 54
Compact fluorescent light bulbs, 64, 71
Composter, 18
Compressor, 59
Conden Saver, 56
Consumer Information Center, 114
Copper, 31
Cornstarch, 36
Cosmetics, 103
Cotton, 19, 102
Cotton diapers, 104
Cotton napkins, 22
Cotton towels, 19
Cream of tartar, 16

D

Deflecto Corp., 63
Deodorant, 106
Deodorizers, 127
Detergent, 20, 21
Dishwasher, 60
Dishwashing liquid, 23
Disinfectants, 24

Double-glazed windows, 62
Drain cleaner, 25
Dry cleaning, 102
Dryer exhaust vent hood, 63
Dryers, 58

E

Eco-Choice, 30
Ecological Water Products, 93
Electronic ballast, 66
Electronic Ballast Technology, 66
Emissions, 54
Energy, 49
Enro Heatsaver, 67
Enro Manufacturing, 67
Ethanol, 36
EveryBody Ltd., 107

F

Fabric softeners, 26
Fan-ventilation system, 56
Faucet aerator, 68
Fertilizer, 18
Fiberglass, 52
Flashlight, 88
Flea repellent, 27
Floor cleaner, 28
Fly swatter, 29
Formaldehyde, 12, 24, 106, 108, 126, 131
Fossil fuels, 58, 55, 111, 112
Friends of the Forest, 128
Fuel efficient car, 114
Furniture, 131
Furniture polish, 30

G

Garden, 11, 18, 41, 90
Gardener's Supply, 18
Gardens Alive, 41
Garlic, 27
Gas appliances, 69
Gas heating system, 81
Gasket insulators, 70
Glass jars, 130
Global warming, 49, 55
Gold, 31

Greeting cards, 123

H

Halogen lighting, 71
Heat traps, 74
Heat-pump heating system, 73
Heating system, 72, 81, 82
Heating system tune-up, 72
Home energy audit, 75
Home Recycling Catalogue, 133
Household, 11, 14
Humane Alternative Products, 33
Hydrocarbons, 15
Hydrochlorofluorocarbon, 34
Hydrogen peroxide, 25

I

Ink stains, 16
Insulated pipes, 74
Intermatic, 80
Isopropyl alcohol, 48

J

Jade Mountain, 15, 88
Janice Corporation, 19

K

Karen's Nontoxic Products, 13, 119
Kim Supply Company, 57

L

Landfills 18, 37, 45, 111, 113, 115, 117, 126, 130
Laundry Powder, 20, 21
Lead, 111, 113, 126
Lemon juice, 16, 30, 42, 46
Lighting, 64, 71, 95
Liquid soap, 16, 23
Live christmas tree, 124
Livos Plantchemistry, 36
Low-flow shower head, 76
Low-flush toilet, 77
Lye, 25, 34

M

Markers, 47
Mercury, 94
Metal polisher, 31
Metals, 132
Microwave oven, 78
Millennium™, 88
Millennium™ recharger, 50
Modulating aquastat, 79
Monkey Globe, 128
Mosquito repellent, 32
Moth balls, 17
Mountain Fresh, 26
Mouse traps, 33

N

Naphtha, 16, 47
Natural deodorant crystal, 106
Natural fibers, 102
Natural soaps, 20
Nigra Enterprises, 23
Nitrobenzene, 42
Non-Scents, 12
Northwoods Nursery, 127
Nuclear power plants, 69

O

Occupancy sensor, 80
Odors, 12
Oil, 103
Oil spills, 49
Olive oil, 30, 42
Oven cleaner, 34
Oxygen, 128

P

Paint, 126
Paint brushes, 125
Paper, 132
Paper Glue, 36
Paper Plates, 37
Paper towels, 19, 38
Peerless Pottery, Inc., 77
Pens, 47
Pentane, 15
*People's Energy Resource
Cooperative*, 71

Perchloroethylene, 102
Pesticides 27, 32, 40
Petroleum products, 31
Phenol, 12, 24, 47, 108, 126
Phosphates, 23
Plants, 127
Plastic, 11, 39, 45, 132
Poison, 33
Polyurethane, 44
Powdered sugar, 40
Power burner, 81

R

Radiator valve, 83
Radioactive waste, 49
Rainforest Action Network, 129
Rainforests, 128
Real Goods Trading Co., 91
Rebuilt engine, 115
Recycled oil change, 116
Recycled paper, 38, 123
Recycling, 37, 45, 122, 132
Refrigerator, 84
Refrigerator brush, 86
Refrigerator door seal, 87
*Resource Conservation
Technology*, 77
Retreaded tires, 117
Rising Sun Enterprises, 68
Roach killer, 40
Rubbermaid™, 39

S

Safecoat paints, 126
Salt, 34
Sea sponges, 44
Seabright Humane Mousetrap, 33
Seasonal Energy Efficiency Rating,
56
Set Point Paper Company, 45
Seventh Generation, 21, 44, 51,
86, 94
Shoe polish, 42
Silk, 102
Silver, 31
Slug Saloon™, 41
Smog, 15, 49, 54, 111
Snail and slug killer, 41

Soap, 108
Sodium hexametaphosphate, 23
Solar Car Corporation, 114
Solar powered flashlight, 88
Space heater, 89
Sponges 44
Squeeze nozzle, 90
Stains, 131
Steel belted tires, 117
Steel wool, 34
Strip mines, 49
Styrene, 37
Styrofoam, 37, 132
Sulfuric acid, 111, 113
Sun Frost, 85
Synthetic fragrances 26, 31, 103
Synthetic materials, 102

T

Talc, 103
Tankless water heater, 91
Television, 92
The Cotton Place, 102
The Ecology Box, 13, 108
The Living Source, 20, 43
The Natural Baby Company, 105
The New Alchemy Institute, 65
Thermal energy, 73
Thermostat, 82
Thermostatic radiator valve, 83
Tires, 117
Toilet, 77
Toilet bowl cleaner, 46
Toilet dam, 93
Toilet paper 38
Toluene, 16, 47
Toxic dumping, 14
Toxic vapors, 14
Trash bags, 45
Trichloroethane, 16
Trichloroethylene, 42
Tune-up, 118
Tungsten-halogen lights, 71

U

Un-petroleum jelly, 109
Unfinished wood furniture, 131

V

Vanpool, 54
Vegetable oil, 28
Ventilation, 12
Vinegar, 16, 25, 28, 30, 34, 42, 48, 125
Vinyl chloride, 36
VitalizeR, 119
Vitamin E, 109
Volta batteries, 50, 94

W

Washing machine, 96
Washing soda, 14
Water 14, 49, 68, 76, 77, 90, 91, 93, 96
Water bed thermostat, 97
Water Conservation Systems 76
Water heater, 74
Water heater insulating blanket, 98
Water soluble pens and markers, 47
Water sources, 49, 124
Water supplies, 113
Weather changes, 79
Weatherstrip, 99
Windows, 62
Window cleaner, 48
Wood pulp cellulose, 44
Wool, 102
Worcestershire Sauce, 31

X

Xylene, 12

Z

Zeolite, 12

About the Green Group

The Green Group is a team of environmentalists, money-conscious consumers, writers and editors seeking to educate the public about contributing to the healing of our hurting planet and saving money. The writers and editors include Barbara Fleishhacker, Patty Friedmann, Loren Werner, Kay Radlauer, and Werner Riefling along with many supportive people and organizations.

Fleishhacker is a mediagenic personality who has been the impetus for rallies on both ecological and animal rights issues in her home state of Mississippi. As proprietor of The Main Attraction in Tupelo, MS, Fleishhacker has pioneered the sale and promotion of environmentally safe products, including natural-fiber clothing, non-toxic cosmetics, and earth-safe cleaning agents.

Friedmann is an earth and money-conscious novelist (*The Exact Image of Mother*, Viking 1991) who made her writing debut with a humor book titled *Too Smart to Be Rich*, which was syndicated by the New York Times.

L.Werner is a Los Angeles based writer and consultant whose articles have appeared in dozens of high-tech magazines. He has been active for many years supporting such environmental groups as Greenpeace, the Nature Conservancy, and several other groups.

Radlauer is the past president of the Louisiana Audobon Society and has served as the Director of the Coalition to Restore Coastal Louisiana.

Riefling is a writer, editor, entrepreneur, environmentalist, and a consummate tightwad.

Order Form

Telephone orders:
Call: **1-800/798-2025** or 504/522-2025.

Have your MasterCard or Visa ready.

Fax orders: 504/891-8316

Postal Orders:

PAPER CHASE PRESS, 5721 Magazine St., Suite 152,
New Orleans, LA, 70115

You can also send all postal correspondences to this address.

Please send _____ copies (indicate quantity of books) of
101 Ways To Save Money & Save Our Planet. Each book
costs $5.95. Call or write to request a discount sheet for
volume purchases exceeding 10 books.

Sales tax:
Please add 9% for books shipped to Louisiana addresses.

Shipping:
Book Rate: $1.75 for the first book and $1.00 for each additional
book. (Surface shipping may take three to four weeks.)
Air Mail: $3 per book.

Payment:

☐ Check

☐ Credit Card: ☐ Visa ☐ MasterCard

Card number: _____

Name on card: _____

Exp. date:_____/_____/_____

Name: _____

Address: _____

_____

_____